D0565068

THANK YOU FOR SMOKING

THANK YOU FOR SMOKING

SCREENPLAY AND INTRODUCTION BY JASON REITMAN

BASED ON THE NOVEL BY CHRISTOPHER BUCKLEY

FOREWORD BY CHRISTOPHER BUCKLEY

A Newmarket Shooting Script® Series Book

NEWMARKET PRESS • NEW YORK

Copyright © 2006 Twentieth Century Fox Film Corporation. All rights reserved.

Foreword copyright © 2007 Christopher Buckley.
Introduction copyright © 2007 Jason Reitman.

All rights reserved. Used by permission.

The Newmarket Shooting Script® Series is a registered trademark of
Newmarket Publishing & Communications Company.

This book is published simultaneously in the United States of America and in Canada.

All rights reserved. This book may not be reproduced, in whole or in part,
in any form, without written permission. Inquiries should be addressed to:
Permissions Department, Newmarket Press, 18 East 48th Street, New York, NY 10017.

FIRST EDITION

10 9 8 7 6 5 4 3 2 1

ISBN: 978-1-55704-775-5

Library of Congress Catalog-in-Publication Data available upon request.

QUANTITY PURCHASES

Companies, professional groups, clubs, and other organizations may qualify for special terms when ordering quantities
of this title. For information, write to Special Sales, Newmarket Press, 18 East 48th Street, New York, NY 10017;
call (212) 832-3575 or 1-800-669-3903; FAX (212) 832-3629; or e-mail info@newmarketpress.com.

Website: www.newmarketpress.com

Manufactured in the United States of America.

OTHER BOOKS IN THE NEWMARKET SHOOTING SCRIPT® SERIES INCLUDE:

About a Boy: The Shooting Script	The Ice Storm: The Shooting Script
Adaptation: The Shooting Script	In Good Company: The Shooting Script
The Age of Innocence: The Shooting Script	Man on the Moon: The Shooting Script
American Beauty: The Shooting Script	The Matrix: The Shooting Script
A Beautiful Mind: The Shooting Script	The People vs. Larry Flynt: The Shooting Script
Big Fish: The Shooting Script	Pieces of April: The Shooting Script
The Birdcage: The Shooting Script	Punch-Drunk Love: The Shooting Script
Black Hawk Down: The Shooting Script	Red Dragon: The Shooting Script
Capote: The Shooting Script	The Shawshank Redemption: The Shooting Script
Cast Away: The Shooting Script	Sideways: The Shooting Script
Cinderella Man: The Shooting Script	Snow Falling on Cedars: The Shooting Script
The Constant Gardener: The Shooting Script	The Squid and the Whale: The Shooting Script
Dead Man Walking: The Shooting Script	State and Main: The Shooting Script
Eternal Sunshine of the Spotless Mind: The Shooting Script	Stranger Than Fiction: The Shooting Script
Gods and Monsters: The Shooting Script	Traffic: The Shooting Script
Gosford Park: The Shooting Script	Transamerica: The Shooting Script
Human Nature: The Shooting Script	The Truman Show: The Shooting Script
	War of the Worlds: The Shooting Script

OTHER NEWMARKET PICTORIAL MOVIEBOOKS AND NEWMARKET INSIDER FILM BOOKS INCLUDE:

The Art of The Matrix*	A Good Year: Portrait of the Film
The Art of X2*	Hitchhiker's Guide to the Galaxy: The Filming of the Douglas Adams Classic
The Art of X-Men: The Last Stand	
Bram Stoker's Dracula: The Film and the Legend*	Hotel Rwanda: Bringing the True Story of an African Hero to Film*
Chicago: The Movie and Lyrics*	The Jaws Log
Dances with Wolves: The Illustrated Story of the Epic Film*	Kinsey: Public and Private*
Dreamgirls	Memoirs of a Geisha: A Portrait of the Film
E.T. The Extra-Terrestrial: From Concept to Classic*	Ray: A Tribute to the Movie, the Music, and the Man*
Gladiator: The Making of the Ridley Scott Epic Film	Saving Private Ryan: The Men, The Mission, The Movie
Good Night, and Good Luck: The Screenplay and History Behind the Landmark Movie*	Schindler's List: Images of the Steven Spielberg Film
	Tim Burton's Corpse Bride: An Invitation to the Wedding

*Includes Screenplay

CONTENTS

FOREWORD

To: Whom It May Concern

From: Christopher Buckley

My phone rang some years ago. It was a then twenty-three-year-old named Jason Reitman on the line. He introduced himself further by saying, "I'm the guy they hired to f— up your book."

The book was a novel called *Thank You for Smoking*. It had been under option, and then was purchased by Icon Productions for Mel Gibson. Ten long years had gone by as it languished in what I believe is called "Development Hell."

I had been shown script after script, with decreasing interest. And then here came this young, eager man, charming me with the first words out of his mouth.

I read the script and immediately realized that my book had fallen into the hands of a seriously talented young artist. Indeed, it was almost as if I were reading the story for the very first time. He had changed it, and yet it was the story I had written. To this day, I don't know how he did it, but I don't question it. I am in respectful awe of his talent.

I remember thinking at the time, Here is the first act in a very bright career. How splendid—how right—it would be if the screenplay were recognized this awards season.

—Christopher Buckley
November 2006

INTRODUCTION

My Experience with the Real Nick Naylor

He looked about 5' 10", in a black Armani suit and a tan that made him resemble above all things a talent agent. Unlike an agent's, however, his smile felt sincere. Most notably, his posture boasted an upright lightness that made him seem . . . guilt-free.

He was the public spokesman for an industry that until recently was perfectly happy to remain a faceless operation, hiding behind characters like Joe Camel and the Marlboro Man. But with cigarette companies folding into much larger food conglomerates and settlements being announced by the day, it was time for Big Tobacco to take the public stage. The grinning man before us worked for Philip Morris, which had recently renamed themselves Altria. (Not kidding.) Apparently Benevolencia and Humanitaria were considered too vulgar.

The evening occurred halfway through a five-year search for financing to direct my screenplay, *Thank You for Smoking*. I was invited to the political equivalent of a heavyweight title fight. Jeff Wigand, the former tobacco executive-turned-informant (most famous for his portrayal by Russell Crowe in the film *The Insider*), was going toe-to-toe with a real-life tobacco spokesman for a live audience.

Wigand spoke first. Now let me preface this by saying that I think Jeff Wigand is an incredible American and one of the bravest men I've ever met. That said, he just might be better suited to standing *up* to Big Tobacco than standing *before* an audience of two hundred people. Even if he reconsidered the disheveled university professor look (elbow patches and all), it would be hard to understand how a man could sweat so much before an audience that was so unanimously supportive.

He flew through his prepared statements, having obviously delivered them before. The statistics, as shocking as they often were, couldn't be fully appreciated due to the rapid way in which they were propelled to the audience. His mind often moved so fast that he would drop words without noticing. He was the best money *couldn't* buy.

The most enjoyable part of all this was watching the tobacco spokesman react to the litany of accusations being launched from the other side of the stage. As the statements got nastier and nastier, the guy in the Armani suit just kept nodding with a compassionate smile. I can only compare it to the way a groom responds to being roasted by his best man at a wedding. If Wigand brought up something like cigarette vending machines at publicly funded day care centers, the spokesman's response would be something akin to, *Yup, that was us. I can't believe you remember that!*

I couldn't help it. I loved this guy. He represented the same charming swagger I fell in love with in Nick Naylor, the lead character of the novel *Thank You for Smoking*. After a half hour of what could only be described as tobacco bashing met by euphoric applause on a religious level, we were introduced to the best money *could* buy. The man in the suit nodded to the audience with a little wave that said, *I know you'd like to lynch me, but perhaps we can have a chat?*

The man from Big Tobacco began talking about Altria's views of the future. None of which were overtly offensive. As you might imagine, he made generous use of the words *freedom, choice,* and *liberty*. He talked so sincerely about putting an end to the segregation of smokers and nonsmokers that I couldn't help wishing he had begun his speech, *I have a dream.*

The highlight of the evening occurred when a seething local man questioned why Big Tobacco was thwarting a new law set to designate California apartment buildings as either smoking or nonsmoking. Again, the spokesman smiled. Then he said:

> *Well, this law is just another example of the rich trying to suppress the poor. Sure, if you're wealthy enough to afford a house, you can choose whether or not to smoke. But if you can't afford a house and are forced to rent, that choice . . . that right is taken away. Well, if there's anything we believe in at Altria, it's freedom. We will not stand by and watch as a person's rights are taken away.*

The answer came off as ridiculous but, to a certain extent, it wasn't that far off from what I believe. I do believe people should have the right to smoke. Just as I believe people should have the right to be stupid, wear Hammer pants, and harm themselves irrevocably if their heart truly desires. The man who asked the question was so stunned by the answer that he just sat back down in confusion. Then the spokesman simply scanned the crowd with a smile for the next questioner.

Toward the end of the evening, I raised my hand. The man from Big Tobacco saw me and pointed me out. A nearby usher brought a micro-phone to my lips. I then asked the man, *Sir, do you have children?* This was a question posed to the main character of my movie, and I wanted to try it out on the real McCoy.

For a split second, the man's smile faded. I understand why. Nothing good could come of this introduction. I was making it personal. No one likes that. But his smile returned and he responded cautiously, *Yes, I'm the proud father of two.*

Just as in my screenplay, I followed up with, *What would you do if you caught them smoking?* He thought about this for a second, then looked back up and said, *I love my children. I want them to be fully aware of the realities of smoking.*

I never spoke to anyone else from Big Tobacco throughout the process of making my film. Jeff Wigand did read the screenplay and offered me plenty of notes, all of them correcting various statistical errors. When I asked him whether he thought it was funny, he responded, *I find the screenplay inaccurate in places.*

—Jason Reitman
November 2006

THANK YOU FOR SMOKING

SCREENPLAY BY
JASON REITMAN

FROM THE NOVEL BY
CHRISTOPHER BUCKLEY

DIRECTED BY
JASON REITMAN

```
BLUE REVISION        1/21/05
SHOOTING DRAFT       1/10/05
```

INT. THE JOAN LUNDEN SHOW SET - DAY

JOAN LUNDEN, America's beloved newswoman and television
personality, stands before her audience. Not just the people
that have waited in line to sit in her presence. Moreover,
the millions of people who will devour each and every word
that leaves her lips.

Sounds daunting. You and I couldn't do it in a million years.
This, however, is what she was born to do. We move across the
PANELISTS as Joan stops at a fifteen year old boy named ROBIN
whose bald head is obviously not a fashion statement.

                    JOAN
          Robin Williger is a fifteen year old
          freshman from Racine, Wisconsin. He likes
          studying history and he's on the debate
          team. Robin's future looked bright,
          however recently, he was diagnosed with
          Cancer. A very tough kind of Cancer.
          Robin tells me he has quit smoking though
          and no longer thinks cigarettes are cool.

Thunderous applause.

Joan moves to NICK NAYLOR... our hero.

                    JOAN
          Nick Naylor is the Vice President of the
          Academy of Tobacco Studies. They are the
          tobacco industry's main lobby in
          Washington, DC and Mr. Naylor is their
          chief spokesman.

Silence.

We are introduced to Nick's fellow panelists in a series of
CAPTIONED STILLS accompanied by SONIC BOOMS.

BOOM! - The "PRESIDENT of MOTHERS AGAINST TEEN SMOKING"...
BOOM! - The "CHAIRWOMAN of THE LUNG ASSOCIATION"...
BOOM! - An "AIDE from HEALTH & HUMAN SERVICES"...
BOOM! - Robin Williger (caption simply reads "CANCER BOY".)

DING! - We land on NICK, whose caption simply reads "ME"

                    NICK (V.O.)
          Few people on this planet know what it is
          to be truly despised.

The scene FREEZES as we switch to Nick's POV of the CROWD. This _is_ a very angry bunch of people. As we pass the FROZEN CROWD, we see PEOPLE: mid-scream, mid-spit, mid-gesture.

                    NICK (V.O.)
          Can you blame them? I earn a living
          fronting an organization that kills one
          thousand two hundred human beings a day.
          Twelve Hundred People. We're talking two
          jumbo jet planeloads a day of men, women,
          and children. I mean there's Caesar,
          Alexander the Great, and me...

FLASH IMAGES (under previous dialogue): 1. CAESAR in the Coliseum 2. ALEXANDER THE GREAT, tromping over the carcases of his enemies 3. NICK NAYLOR holding out a light to the audience in front of the American flag.

                    NICK (V.O.)
          ...Nick Naylor. The face of cigarettes.
          The Colonel Sanders of Nicotine.

EXT. ACADEMY OF TOBACCO STUDIES - DAY

A collegiate style brick building with no distinct features, featuring a yellow sign: THE ACADEMY OF TOBACCO STUDIES

                    NICK (V.O.)
          This is where I work. The Academy of
          Tobacco Studies. It was established by
          seven gentlemen you may recognize from C-
          Span...

FLASH IMAGES: The seven Tobacco CEO's testifying in Congress.

                    NICK (V.O.)
          These guys realized quick, if they were
          going to claim that cigarettes were not
          addictive, they better have proof...

INT. LAB - ACADEMY OF TOBACCO STUDIES - DAY

ERHARDT VON GRUPPEN-MUNDT, an older scientist who "escaped" from Germany. His lapel reads "scientist-in-residence". He signals a lab tech who presses a button on a machine linked to a glass cage of mice. Immediately, it fills with smoke.

                    NICK (V.O.)
          This is the man they rely on, Erhardt Von
          Gruppen-Mundt. They found him in Germany.
          I won't go into the details.
                    (MORE)

                    NICK (V.O.) (CONT'D)
          He's been testing the link between
          nicotine and lung cancer for thirty years
          and hasn't found any conclusive results.
          The man is a genius. He could disprove
          gravity.

INT. LAW LIBRARY - ACADEMY OF TOBACCO STUDIES - DAY

Twenty KILLER LAWYERS sit around a conference table,
devouring law books and journals.

                    NICK (V.O.)
          Then, we've got our sharks. We draft them
          out of Ivy League law schools and give
          them sports cars and time shares. It's
          just like a John Grisham novel without
          all the espionage.

INT. RECEPTION - ACADEMY OF TOBACCO STUDIES - DAY

A mix of red and yellow wood paneling makes the place
actually look like a cigarette carton.

                    NICK (V.O.)
          Most importantly, we've got spin control.
          That's where I come in. I get paid to
          talk. I don't have an MD or a law degree.
          I've got a bachelors in kicking ass and
          taking names.

INT. PRESS CONFERENCE (BLACK LIMBO) - DAY

Nick's head turns towards us in SLO-MO. As his mouth opens to
speak, we ramp into SUPER-SPEED, sending his mouth to 100 WPS
(words per second). Nick expels syllables like bullets to the
sound of an M-16 emptying a full clip.

                    NICK (V.O.)
          You know that guy who can pick up any
          girl?

EXT. BASEBALL DIAMOND - NIGHT

Nick is at the plate in rolled up sleeves and a tie. He
clicks the bat against his loafers. There's the pitch. He
swings, connects, home run.

                    NICK (V.O.)
          I'm him on crack.

                                        BACK TO:

INT. JOAN LUNDEN SHOW SOUND STAGE - DAY

Joan continues with her introduction...

>   JOAN
>   Obviously, this is a very heated issue
>   and I'd like to cover as much as...

Joan notices that Nick is raising his hand, bringing
uncertainty to his fellow panelists.

>   JOAN (CONT'D)
>   (smiling)
>   Yes, Nick? You have a question?

>   NICK
>   Joan, how on earth would big tobacco
>   profit off of the loss of this young man?
>   (Nick places his hand on
>   Robin's shoulder)
>   I hate to think in such callous terms, but
>   if anything we'd be losing a customer. It's
>   not only our hope but it's in our best
>   interests to keep Robin alive and smoking.

Joan raises an eyebrow.

>   RON GOODE
>   That's ludicrous!

>   NICK
>   Let me tell you something Joan, and let
>   me share something with the fine,
>   concerned people in the audience today.
>   The Ron Goode's of this world *want* the
>   Robin Willigers to die.

>   RON GOODE
>   What?!

>   NICK
>   (Clenches Robin's shoulder)
>   Awful, but true. I'm sorry, but it's a
>   fact. And do you know why?

Joan raises her palm, awaiting Nick's answer.

>   NICK (CONT'D)
>   I'll tell you why. So that their *budgets*
>   will go up.
>   (MORE)

                    NICK (CONT'D)
This is nothing less than trafficking in
human misery, and you, sir, ought to be
ashamed of yourself.

                    RON GOODE
          (flabbergasted)
I should be ashamed of myself?!

                    NICK
          (compassionately)
As a matter of fact, we're about to
launch... a fifty-million-dollar campaign
aimed at persuading kids not to smoke.
Because I think we can all agree that
nothing is more important than America's
children.

                    JOAN
And with that, we'll have to take a short
break. Hang on, there's much more to come.

                    TECHNICIAN
And we're out!

Joan exhales. She gives Nick a long stare. Almost impressed.
Nick smiles back, then takes a sip of water.

                                        CUT TO:

EXT. JOAN LUNDEN THEATRE - LOS ANGELES - DAY

Nick steps out of a backstage door onto the sidewalk and into
a waiting LIMOUSINE, while answering his ringing CELL PHONE
in one movement.

INT. LIMOUSINE - SAME

Nick is swallowed by the plush black leather.

                    NICK
          (answering phone)
     Yes?

                              CONTINUE INTERCUT WITH:

INT. BR'S OFFICE - ACADEMY OF TOBACCO STUDIES - DAY

BR, Nick's boss and a real shit kicker, fumes into the receiver.

                    BR (O.S.)
Fifty million dollars... are you out of
your fucking mind?!

                              NICK (V.O.)
          Everyone has a boss... BR just happens to
          be mine.

                                                  FLASH TO:

INT. SQUASH COURT - DAY

BR enters the court and begins to hit the ball. He is a tall
man with strong features in his forties. Stained headband.

                              NICK (V.O.)
          He came from the vending machine world.
          This made him tough.

BR is at full speed. He slams his opponent into the wall.

                              NICK (V.O.) (CONT'D)
          The name, BR, came from his tour in
          Vietnam. The five people who know it's
          meaning are all dead.

FLASH IMAGE - A B&W PHOTO of BR's platoon. Every face is
"X"ed out in red slashes but his.

                                                  BACK TO:

INT. BR'S OFFICE - ACADEMY OF TOBACCO STUDIES - CONTINUED

                              BR
          The deal was five million.

                              NICK
          Five million dollars will buy you a
          couple subway posters. It's not going to
          impress anyone.

                              BR
          That's the idea, Nick.

                              NICK
          You'll be thanking me soon. This will
          probably get you great press.

                              BR
          I got to call the Captain and see if this
          is going to fly. Get your ass back to DC.

EXT. DC SKYLINE - DAY

A plane descends comes into Regan National over Jefferson.

EXT. THE POTOMIC - DAY

Nick's BMW flies over the bridge into the city.

EXT. SAINT EUTHANASIUS MIDDLE SCHOOL - DAY

Nick comes screeching up in his BMW 540.

INT. SCHOOL HALLWAY - DAY

Nick sits on a short school bench, clasping his hands as he
waits. We pull out to reveal a PILOT in full uniform sitting
next to him. They share a nod. Nick lets out a little "hmm".

A TEACHER opens a door nearby and sticks her head out.

>   TEACHER
>   Mr. Naylor, it's your turn.

Nick stands and fixes his tie as a FIREMAN, in full gear,
steps out of the door. Again, Nick and the man share a nod.

>   TEACHER (CONT'D)
>   (to Nick)
>   Joey is such a bright young man. We all
>   look forward to him coming out of his
>   shell a little. He's a bit shy.

>   NICK
>   He gets that from his mother.

The teacher lets out a little "oh" as Nick enters...

INT. CLASSROOM - DAY

A BANNER hung across the chalkboard reads: *"WHAT DO YOU DO?"*
Nick enters the classroom and proceeds towards the front. He
briefly stops at the desk of his twelve year old son, JOEY.

>   NICK
>   Hey, there.

>   JOEY
>   (whispering)
>   *Please don't ruin my childhood.*

Nick nods reassuringly, pats him on the head, then continues
to the front. For a beat, he takes in a giant breath, trying
to swallow all the oxygen in the room. Then, he begins:

                    NICK
          How many of you want to be lawyers when
          you grow up?

One hand. A real prick of a kid.

                    NICK
          How about movie stars?

Almost every hand in the room goes up.

                    NICK
          How about lobbyists?

                    KID 1
          What's that?

                    NICK
          It's kind of like being in the movies.
          It's what I do. I talk for a living.

                    KID 2
          What do you talk about?

                    NICK
          I speak on behalf of cigarettes.

Gasps around the room. Joey looks around in growing fear.

                    KID 3
          My mom used to smoke. She says that
          cigarettes kill.

                    NICK
               (to Kid 3)
          Really? Is your mom a doctor?

                    KID 3
          No.

                    NICK
               (to Kid 3)
          A scientific researcher of some kind?

                    KID 3
          No.

                    NICK
          Well, she doesn't exactly sound like a
          credible expert now does she?

Kid 3 sinks in his seat.

                    NICK
          Don't feel bad. It's okay to listen to
          your mom.
               (winking at Joey)
          I mean, it's good to listen to your
          parents.
               (to the class)
          All I'm suggesting is that there will
          always be people trying to tell you what to
          do and what to think. There probably
          already are people doing that. Am I right?

Nods across the classroom. The teacher is a little skittish.

                    NICK (CONT'D)
          I'm here to say that when someone tries
          to act like some sort of expert, you can
          respond, "who says?"

                    KID 4
          So cigarettes are good for you?

                    TEACHER
               (quickly)
          No...

                    NICK
          ... No, that's not what I'm getting at. My
          point is you have to think for yourself.
               (bangs a desk)
          Challenge authority!

A couple kids gasp.

                    NICK (CONT'D)
          If your parents told you that chocolate
          was dangerous, would you just take their
          words for it?

                    THE WHOLE CLASS
          Noooo.

                    NICK
          Exactly. So, perhaps instead of acting
          like sheep, when it comes to cigarettes,
          you should find out for yourself.

                         TEACHER
                 (steps in front of Nick)
            Okay, then... Thank you Mr. Naylor for
            joining us...

Joey and his dad meet eyes. Nick gives a little, *"How'd I
do?"* motion. Joey drops his head in embarrassment.

INT. BERT'S RESTAURANT - DAY

Dark. Especially the corner that Nick's table occupies. Nick
is seated with his closest friends. The only people who
understand. BOBBY JAY BLISS, a larger than life gun advocate
from Loober, Mississippi and POLLY BAILEY, an attractive
alcohol lobbyist with a quick tongue.

                         NICK (V.O.)
            Every week, we meet here at Bert's.
            Together, we represent the chief
            spokespeople for the Tobacco, Alcohol,
            and Firearms industries.

We see ICONS of a GUN, BOTTLE, and CIGARETTE pop up over each
corresponding MOD squad member's head.

                         NICK (V.O.)
            We call ourselves the Mod Squad. M-O-D.
            Merchants of Death.

                         POLLY
            So, my day is ruined.

                         NICK
            Why?

                         POLLY
            Dateline is doing a segment on fetal
            alcohol syndrome. *Thank you.*

FREEZE ON POLLY

                         NICK (V.O.)
            Polly works for The Moderation Council.

FLASH IMAGE: The Moderation Council LOGO - A mother eagle
proudly feeding her young with bottles of whiskey and gin.

                         NICK (V.O.)
            A casual drinker by the age of
            fourteen...

FLASH IMAGE: POLLY'S HEADSHOT

In the moderation conference room, surrounded by men in bad
suits, each pointing various bottles of alcohol at her.

                    NICK (V.O.)
          ... Polly developed a tolerance usually
          reserved for Irish dockworkers.

FLASH IMAGE: INT. MODERATION COUNCIL PRESS CONFERENCE - DAY

Polly speaks with ease and confidence. A flashbulb pops us
into the cover of the trade magazine - "The Daily Drinker."

                    NICK (V.O.)
          In our world, she's the woman who got the
          Pope to endorse red wine.

The tag reads "Mother Burgundy!"

                                             BACK TO:

INT. BERT'S RESTAURANT - CONTINUED

                    POLLY
          We're going to get creamed. Any ideas?

                    NICK
          I don't know. Deformed kids are tough.
          I'm lucky. My product only makes them
          bald before it kills them.

                    BOBBY JAY
          Maybe you could hug the kids.

                    POLLY
          They're not going to let me *hug* the kids.

                    NICK
          Who's doing the segment? Donaldson or
          Sawyer?

                    POLLY
          Sawyer, probably.

                    BOBBY JAY
          You're fucked.

                    POLLY
          Why?

                    NICK
          She's going to hug them.

                    BOBBY JAY
          Look, if you see her going in for a hug,
          maybe you can try to box her out and get
          one before she does.

Bobby Jay is demonstrating the "Box-Out", when he FREEZES.

                    NICK (V.O.)
          Bobby Jay works for SAFETY.

FLASH IMAGE: The Safety SHIELD - An Eagle with a RIFLE.

                    NICK
          The Society for the Advancement of
          Firearms and Effective Training of Youth.

INT. PHOTO STUDIO - DAY

Bobby Jay poses for his head shot, with a large rifle.

                    BOBBY JAY
          You want me to smile?

He laughs then suddenly get serious with his gun.

FLASH IMAGE: The Kent State Shootings.

                    NICK (V.O.)
          After watching the footage of the Kent
          State shootings, Bobby Jay, then
          seventeen, signed up for the National
          Guard, so that he too could shoot college
          students...

FLASH IMAGE: NATIONAL GUARD RECRUITER'S DOOR:

A sign reads... "Be back in ten... To ENLIST more men!"

                    NICK (V.O.)
          But the National Guard recruiter was out
          to lunch so Bobby Jay ended up shooting
          Panamanians instead...

FLASH IMAGE: EXT. JUNGLE - DAY

Bobby Jay steps out of the jungle in full camo with a rifle.
Subtitle read: "OPERATION JUST CAUSE".

                              NICK
          ...which was almost as good as college
          students, only they shoot back.

Bobby Jay takes a SHOT in the arm. He looks confused.

                                        BACK TO:

INT. BERT'S RESTAURANT - DAY

                              BOBBY JAY
          You know you can beat a breathalyzer by
          sucking on activated charcoal tablets.

                              POLLY
          Well perhaps we should change our
          campaign to "If you must drink and drive,
          suck charcoal."

                              NICK
          But don't the police wonder why you're
          sucking on charcoal?

                              BOBBY JAY
          There's no law against charcoal.

                              ALL THREE
          YET!

INT. DINING ROOM - NICK'S APARTMENT - NIGHT

Nick and Joey sit at opposite ends of the DINING ROOM TABLE,
doing their respective homework.

Nick is HIGHLIGHTING lines from various briefs.

Joey is trying to write an essay. Pencil on paper. Joey stops
for a moment. He looks up at his father.

                              JOEY
          Dad, why is American government, the best
          government?

                              NICK
                   (without looking)
          Because of our endless appeals system.

Joey goes back to writing. Nick suddenly looks up and
realizes what he's done.

                    NICK
          Joey, you're not writing down what I just
          said, are you?

Joey nods YES.

                    NICK
          Stop for a second.

Joey drops his pencil.

                    NICK
          What is the subject of your essay?

                    JOEY
          Why is the American government the best
          government in the world?

                    NICK
          Your teacher crafted that question?

                    JOEY
          Yeah. Why?

                    NICK
          Well, for the moment, I'll look past the
          obvious problems in syntax and focus more
          on the core of the question.

Joey rolls his eyes. He's heard this before.

                    NICK (CONT'D)
          I mean, A. Does America have the best
          government? and B. What constitutes a
          best government? Crime? Poverty?
          Literacy? In America? Definitely not
          best. Perhaps not even better than most.
               (however)
          We do have a very entertaining
          government.

                    JOEY
          Dad?

                    NICK
          Sorry.
               (back to being a father)
          Joey, are you familiar with the term,
          B.S.?

                    JOEY
              (matter of fact)
     Bullshit?

                    NICK
     Yes. Exactly. B.S., if I may, is what
     questions like the one your teacher posed
     are made for. Even if America had the
     best government, there'd be no way to
     prove it in... how many pages are you
     writing?

                    JOEY
     Two pages.

                    NICK
     Definitely not in two pages.

                    JOEY
     So what am I supposed to write?

                    NICK
     Whatever you want.

                    JOEY
              (elaborate)
     Okay?

                    NICK
     Write about America's amazing ability to
     make profit by breaking down trading
     tariffs and bringing American jobs to
     third world countries or how good we are
     at executing felons. They're all correct
     answers.

                    JOEY
     I can do that?

                    NICK
     Oh Joey, that's the beauty of argument.
     If you argue correctly, you're never
     wrong.

A whole new world opens in Joey's eyes.

Nick goes back to his work.

                    JOEY
     Dad, if I finish the essay within an
     hour, can we stay up all night?

                    NICK
               (without looking up)
          That's a negotiation, not an argument.

INT. NICK'S APARTMENT - LATER THAT NIGHT

Nick intently watches THE SANDS OF IWO JIMA. Joey has already
fallen asleep next to him.

On TV - John Wayne, having brought his men through hell to
victory, gives them the post game speech.

                    JOHN WAYNE
          ...I never felt so good in my life. How
          about a cigarette?

Just as he's offering the pack around to his men, a Japanese
sniper drills him, dead.

Without realizing it, Nick takes out a cigarette PACK. He
reaches for a smoke, but the pack is empty. Nick looks back
at John Wayne, then back at his Cigarette Pack. Nick smiles.
He's got something.

EXT. BEAUTIFUL SUBURBAN COTTAGE - MONDAY MORNING

Nick and Joey walk up to the door. It opens, revealing Nick's
ex-wife JILL. Joey scurries past his mother into the house.

                    JILL
          You still own a watch, don't you Nick?

                    NICK
          Jill, I can't help feeling that Joey is
          getting the wrong idea about his father.
          It would be great if I could spend a
          little more time with him. You know, to
          give him a fair and balanced perspective.

                    JILL
          Nick, you had plenty of time for that.
          Now you're his weekend guardian. Besides,
          he has Brad.

                    NICK
          He still needs a father.

On cue, BRAD steps through the door between them. Brad is
Nick's taller and broader replacement. He's an MD, and he's
wearing the WHITE COAT and BADGE to prove it.

                    BRAD
          Nick, you got a second?

                    NICK
          Sure, Brad.

Brad walks Nick back to his car.

                    BRAD
          Nick, your job and everything aside, I
          hope you understand that second hand
          smoke is a real killer.

                    NICK
          What are you talking about?

                    BRAD
          I just hope you keep Joey in a smoke free
          environment. That's all I'm saying.

                    NICK
          Brad, I'm his father. You're the guy
          fucking his mom.

Nick gets into his car.

                    BRAD
          That's just unnecessary.

                                             CUT TO:

EXT. PRESS CONFERENCE, PULMONARY COUNCIL LOBBY - DAY

ON C-SPAN. The man at the podium is SENATOR FINISTIRRE and by
the chyron along the bottom of the screen, we can see he is a
(D) from Vermont. Behind him are a man in a lab coat and the
Surgeon General, medals et al.

                    FINISTIRRE
          Tobacco is winning the war. The war on
          our children. They like to use symbols
          and cartoons to get our kids hooked.
          Well, we have a symbol of our own...

Finistirre pulls back a curtain, revealing a SKULL & CROSSBONES.

                    FINISTIRRE (CONT'D)
          It is my hope that by the end of the
          year, all cigarette packages sold in the
          United States will carry this emblem.
                    (MORE)

FINISTIRRE (CONT'D)
Perhaps then cigarettes will finally be
labeled appropriately - as poison. I will
be holding a congressional hearing to
discuss the inclusion of the skull and
crossbones in two weeks time. As usual, I
send an open invitation to Big Tobacco to
come and join us. Perhaps, this time they
will grace us with their presence and
their answers.

Flashbulbs. Commotion.

We pop out of the screen to reveal we are in...

INT. CONFERENCE ROOM - ACADEMY OF TOBACCO STUDIES - DAY

The Spin Control team sits around the long oval table.
Somewhere in the middle sits Nick. His eyelids drop to half
mast in reaction to the video.

NICK (V.O.)
Prick.

BR freezes the MONITOR on Finistirre's clammy face. He then
grabs the top of the conference table with his opens palms.

The fifteen or so people in suits prepare for a beating.

BR
People. What is going on out there? I
look down this table, and all I see are
white flags. Our numbers are down all
across the board. Teen smoking, our bread
and butter, is falling like a shit from
heaven. We don't sell Tic-Tacs for
Christ's sakes. We sell cigarettes. And
they're cool, and available, and
addictive. The job is almost done for us.
(pointing back to Finistirre's
frozen face)
This "environmentalist"...

As BR says this, the word "PUSSY" appears below as a translation.

BR
... is challenging us. We have to have an
answer. I'm asking you - When this
cocksucker puts Captain Hook on our
product, what are we going to do?

NICK
BR?

                    BR
          Yeah, Nick?

                    NICK
          If I may?

BR gives the look of *By all means, impress me.*

Nick stands and begins to circle the large table.

                    NICK
          In 1910 the US was producing ten billion
          cigarettes a year. By 1930, we were up to
          one hundred twenty three billion. What
          happened in between?

Blank stares all around.

                    NICK
          Three things. A World War. Dieting. And
          Movies.

                    BR
          Movies?

                    NICK
          1927. Talking pictures are born. Suddenly
          directors need to give their actors
          something to do when they're talking.
          Cary Grant and Carole Lombard are
          lighting up. Bette Davis - a chimney. And
          Bogart! Remember the first picture with
          him and Lauren Bacall?

                    BR
          Not specifically.

                    NICK
               (imitating Bacall)
          She sort of shimmies in through the
          doorway, nineteen years old, pure sex.
          She says, "Anybody got a match?"
               (back to being Nick)
          And Bogie throws the matches at her...

Nick tosses a book of matches to an attractive young lobbyist.

                    NICK
          ...And she catches them. Greatest romance
          of the century and how did it start?
          Lighting a cigarette.
               (MORE)

> NICK (CONT'D)
> (switches gears)
> These days when someone smokes in a
> movie, they're either a psychopath or...
> (even worse)
> ... European.

Nick goes in for the kill.

> NICK
> The message Hollywood needs to send out
> is, *Smoking is Cool*. We need the cast of
> *Will & Grace* smoking in their living
> room. Forrest Gump puffing away between
> his box of chocolates. Hugh Grant earning
> back the love of Julia Roberts by buying
> her favorite brand... *her Virginia Slims*.
> Most of the actors smoke already. If they
> start doing it on screen, we can put the
> sex back into cigarettes.

Nick feels like taking a bow, but he'll settle for a seat.

> BR
> Well, it's a thought. I was hoping for
> something a little more inspiring, but at
> least you're thinking. People, slam your
> fucking brains against your desks until
> something useful comes out.

BR stands and the meeting is over. As people leave, BR
motions to Nick. On the way over, a TRAINEE stops him.

> TRAINEE
> That was awesome.

> NICK
> Hey, thanks.

Nick stops at BR.

> BR
> Nick, you've been summoned. The Captain
> wants to see you.

> NICK
> He saw Joan? What did he think?

> BR
> Get your ass on the next flight to
> Winston-Salem.

INT. BOEING 767 - DAY

We hover over FIRST CLASS, but Nick isn't there.

> NICK (V.O.)
> Could I afford to sit in First?

Still hovering over the cabin we begin to move towards the tail of the plane.

> NICK (V.O.)
> Of course I could.

We cross into BUSINESS CLASS.

> NICK (V.O.)
> Business Class? Hell, I could just bump
> up. I've got enough frequent flyer miles
> to ride in the cockpit.

We cross into COACH.

> NICK (V.O.)
> I like to ride with the people.

We stop on the worst seat in the plane. Center Seat. Five rows from the back. Nick is crammed in between a college baseball team in uniform.

> NICK (V.O.)
> Know your clients. My people cram
> themselves into a tiny seat, take a Xanax
> and dream of the moment they can stuff
> their face with fresh tobacco.

The Team starts tossing around a ball. Nick is unfazed.

> NICK (V.O.)
> If I can convince just one of these kids
> to pick up smoking, I've paid for my
> flight round trip.

Nick greets the kid next to him.

> CUT TO:

INT. MAIN DINING ROOM - THE TOBACCO CLUB - SAME

One word: mahogany. Old white members. Young black waiters.

                    NICK (V.O.)
          The Captain is the last great men of
          tobacco. He introduced filters when
          cigarettes first got slammed by Reader's
          Digest. Later, he founded the Academy of
          Tobacco Studies.

Nick follows the host down stairs into a smoke filled room.

                    NICK (V.O.)
          The Club was founded by the Tobacco
          Barons in 1890, so they would have a
          place to get away from their wives.

Nick follows the host through curtains into various rooms
where men sip liquor and play cards.

                    NICK (V.O.)
          Here, the captain is a legend. A self-
          made man, who started from nothing and
          ended with everything. Except, evidently,
          a son.

The host leads Nick through one final curtain. Behind which
is a man in a double breasted summer suit, seated in a
leather chair that could only be described as a pleated
thrown. This is the CAPTAIN.

                    CAPTAIN
          Nick, my boy. Just in time for mud.

Nick sits down as a WAITER arrives with MINT JULEPS.

Both take sips and "aaah".

                    CAPTAIN
          Do you know the secret to a *really* good
          julep? Crush the mint down onto the ice
          with your thumb and grind it in. Release
          the menthol.
              (demonstrates)
          You know who taught me that?

Nick shrugs "no".

                    CAPTAIN
          Fidel Castro.

The Captain takes another sip.

                    CAPTAIN
          Do you remember Nineteen-Fifty-Two?

                    NICK
          Sir, I wasn't alive in Nineteen-Fifty-Two.

                    CAPTAIN
          Good Lord. I was in Korea shooting
          Chinese in Nineteen-Fifty-Two.

                    NICK
               (not a question)
          Really.

                    CAPTAIN
          Today, they're our best customer.
               (chuckle)
          Next time, we won't have to shoot so many
          of'em, will we?

The waiter appears with another round of Juleps.

                    CAPTAIN
          Nineteen-Fifty-Two was the year Readers
          Digest nailed us with the whole health...
          aspect. As Churchill said, That was
          perhaps *the end of our beginning*.

The Captain takes a long sip.

                    CAPTAIN
          Do you *enjoy* your current work, Nick?

                    NICK
          Yes, it's challenging. If you can do
          Tobacco, you can do anything.

The Captain smiles at this.

                    CAPTAIN
          You know Nick, you remind me just a
          little bit of myself when I was your age.

                    NICK
          Thank you sir.

                    CAPTAIN
          Tell me, what is your opinion of BR?

                    NICK
          BR is... my boss.

                    CAPTAIN
          BR's come under the idea that we should
          start bribing Producers in Hollywood to
          make their actors smoke on screen.

It takes every part of Nick's strength to not verbally
dismantle BR right there and then.

                    NICK
          Say, that's a great idea.

                    CAPTAIN
          Smart man, that BR.

                    NICK
          Oh yeah, and loyal.

                                        CUT TO:

EXT. THE US CAPITAL BUILDING - DAY

There she stands, one of the most powerful structures in the
world. Think how many laws are being broken inside right now.

                                        CUT TO:

SENATOR FINISTIRRE'S DOOR:

SENATOR FINISTIRRE VERMONT

INT. SENATOR FINISTIRRE'S OFFICE - DAY

Oak desk lined with glass jars of maple syrup. US and Vermont
FLAGS. A giant plastic cheese in the shape of Vermont, that
reads, "Vermont, where the cheddar is better."

Push in on Senator FINISTIRRE, as Ron Goode from the Joan
Lunden show enters the room.

                    FINISTIRRE
                 (not looking up)
          Have a seat, Ron.

Ron sits down, apprehensively. He's obviously scared.

                    FINISTIRRE (CONT'D)
          You see Ron, I can't be everywhere I'm
          needed. That's why I send people like you
          to speak on my behalf. When you're there,
          you're not Ron Goode, the guy your
          friends may like.
                    (MORE)

FINISTIRRE (CONT'D)
You're Senator Finistirre's Aide and your name really doesn't matter. So when Ron Goode is a complete asshole on the Joan Lunden show... I am being an asshole on the Joan Lunden show.

RON GOODE
Senator, sir, he just sprang on me like an animal. I couldn't get a word in.

FINISTIRRE
Where the hell did you find cancer boy?

RON GOODE
He was supposed to be very reliable. The Pulmonary Council was one of his references.

FINISTIRRE
    (to himself)
Fucking non-profits.
    (back to Ron)
When you're looking for a cancer kid, he should be hopeless. He should have a wheelchair. He should have trouble speaking. He should have a pet goldfish that he carries around in a little ziplock bag. Hopeless. He should not have a sense of humor.

RON GOODE
I apologize Senator. But if it wasn't for Nick Naylor...

FINISTIRRE
Nick Naylor? Don't even think of using that as an excuse. The man shills bullshit for a living. You work for a fucking Senator. A Senator who is supposed to be tough on Tobacco. Have a little pride.

RON GOODE
It won't happen again, sir.

FINISTIRRE
Alright, you're excused.

EXT. WINSTON-SALEM COUNTRY SIDE - DAY

The Captain's WHITE ROLLS ROYCE LIMO zips by.

INT. THE CAPTAIN'S LIMO - DAY

Nick and the Captain sit across from each other.

                  CAPTAIN
        Sometimes I feel like a Columbian Drug
        Dealer. The other day, my own
        granddaughter, flesh of flesh of my own
        loins, asked me 'Granddaddy, is it true
        cigarettes are *bad* for you?'
           (back to Nick)
        We got to do something, Nick. I think
        you're our man.

                  NICK
        Thank you, sir.

                  CAPTAIN
        I want you to work on this Hollywood
        project. Get out there. Stir things up.
        Report directly to me.

                  NICK
           (hesitant)
        Sir, about the... The fifty million
        dollars...

                  CAPTAIN
        Oh, in anti-teen smoking advertising?
           (chuckles)
        Well, shit, I sure hope it's not too
        persuasive.
           (chuckles)
        I hope.

EXT. WINSTON-SALEM AIRPORT - DAY

The Captain's Limo pulls into a private gate and stops in
front of a FALCON 900. Nick gets out of the Limo.

                  CAPTAIN
        Nick, you're family now. Tobacco takes
        care of its own.

And with that, the Captain slips back into his Limo.

INT. FALCON 900 - SAME

Nick climbs aboard and is shocked by the lavish interior. He
is greeted by TIFFANY, a gorgeous STEWARDESS.

                    TIFFANY
          Mr. Naylor? Welcome to Tobacco One.

Nick melts into a seat of creamy brown leather.

                    TIFFANY (CONT'D)
          The captain told me to take extra special
          care of you, so if there's anything at all
          I can do to make your flight more pleasant,
          you be *sure* to let me know, now.

     WE HEAR THE SOUND OF THE JET TAKING FLIGHT AS WE FADE TO:

INT. DIXIE SLIMS POSTER - ACADEMY TOBACCO STUDIES - DAY

We pull out, then Nick walks by on the way to his office.

INT. NICK'S OFFICE - ACADEMY OF TOBACCO STUDIES - DAY

Nick takes a seat at his desk as GIZELLE, his assistant,
follows with his "While You Were Outs".

                    GIZELLE
               (handing over messages)
          You've got a lot of new fans.

Nick begins to go through the MESSAGES.

                    NICK
               (reading a couple)
          *I'm going to pour hot tar down your
          throat, you scumbag... I own a high-
          powered rifle and could drop a sack of
          shit like you at 250 yards.*
               (to Gizelle)
          You wrote death threats down on message
          slips?

                    GIZELLE
          Until I ran out of paper.
               (continues)
          Everyone from *Newsweek* to *Teen People*
          want to talk to you. Heather Holloway
          from the paper left five messages. Oh,
          and BR wants to see you.

INT. BR'S OFFICE - ACADEMY OF TOBACCO STUDIES - DAY

As Nick enters, BR welcomes him with a grunt.

                    BR
          Pleasant flight?

                    NICK
          Oh, yeah, you could say that.

BR raises an eyebrow.

                    NICK
          I came up on the Captain's plane. Quite
          the way to travel.

                    BR
          I wouldn't know.

                    NICK
               (digging it in)
          Oh, you've never been on the plane, with
          those seats, and the kitchen, and that
          stewardess. Tiffany.

                    BR
          I haven't had the chance yet.

                    NICK
               (deeper)
          Oh, well, you really must try it
          sometime. It's the only way to travel.

BR is quick to stop this.

                    BR
          What did he think of the fifty million
          dollar anti-smoking campaign?

                    NICK
          Anti-teen smoking campaign. He gave me
          the go ahead. Oh, and he loved your idea
          to put cigarettes back into movies.

                    BR
               (covering up)
          That's your idea. He must have gotten
          confused.

                    NICK
          Either way, he was pretty blown away.

                    BR
          Right, well, get a ticket to LA. I'll get
          you a meeting with Jeff Megall.

                    NICK
               (getting up)
     Who?

                    BR
     Hollywood super-agent. Runs the agency,
     E-G-O. Entertainment Global Offices. He <u>is</u>
     the entertainment business.

INT. NICK'S OFFICE - DAY

Nick is on the phone with his ex-wife, JILL.

                    NICK
     It's not a vacation. It's a learning
     experience. California is one of the
     fastest growing states. It has the
     largest number of electoral votes in the
     country. This could be an important trip
     for Joey.

INTERCUT WITH:

INT. JILL'S KITCHEN - DAY

Jill is on the phone, while Joey does his homework at the
kitchen table, pretending not to listen.

                    JILL
     Don't smooth talk me. You're not going to
     take him sight-seeing. You'll probably
     bring him to some lung cancer symposium
     where a guy with an electronic voice box
     will tell him his father is the devil.

                    NICK
     That's unfair.

                    JILL
     Unfair? What about Virginia?

                    NICK
     What about Virginia?

                    JILL
     You took him to a cigarette factory.

                    NICK
     It was a tobacco farm. Hardly the same
     thing.

                         JILL
          This conversation is over.

Jill hangs up.

Nick closes the cell phone against his chest.

                         NICK
          Fuck.

                                             CUT TO:

INT. BERT'S RESTAURANT - DAY

The MOD Squad is in their usual corner.

                         BOBBY JAY
          Last week, we had another disgruntled
          postman. Of course, within the hour, I
          got the Washington Post calling me on the
          phone. Godless swine! I said to them,
          when a plane crashes on account of pilot
          error do you blame the Boeing
          Corporation?

                         POLLY
          Nice one.

                         NICK
          That's good.

                         BOBBY JAY
          Thank you. When some booze-besotten drunk
          goes and runs someone down, do you go
          banging on the door of General Motors?

                         POLLY
          Tell me you didn't say that.

Bobby Jay half apologizes with a grunt, but all is fair in
the world of spin. Nick breaks the moment.

                         NICK
          Do either of you know anything about this
          reporter, Heather Holloway?

                         BOBBY JAY
          Oh yeah. Irish type, brown hair, big blue
          eyes, great skin. Amazing tits.

                    POLLY
          Tits? Why are tits relevant?

                    BOBBY JAY
          Hmm, let's see. World class tits on a
          reporter interviewing a man with
          privileged information are relevant.

                    POLLY
          How about it Nick? Are you a "tit" man?

                    BOBBY JAY
          Don't answer that. That's a trap.

                    NICK
          It depends, whose tits?

Polly smiles. Nick smiles back.

                    BOBBY JAY
          Okay, yeah, just don't get screwed.

                    NICK
          Bobby, I think I can handle a good-
          looking girl reporter.

                                        CUT TO:

INT. IL PECCATORE RESTAURANT - EARLY EVENING

One word: Burgundy.

Nick walks right past the reservation desk. When he reaches
his regular booth, it is already occupied by HEATHER
HOLLOWAY. She stands to greet Nick. Heather is everything you
thought she'd be... in a great skirt.

                    HEATHER
          Heather Holloway.

                    NICK
          Nick Naylor, Big Tobacco.

Heather places a tape recorder on the table as she sits.

                    HEATHER
               (re: tape recorder)
          Is this kosher?

                    NICK
          Only if I can call you Heather.

                    HEATHER
          By all means. So, Mr. Naylor...

                    NICK
          Nick...

                    HEATHER
               (all business)
          Nick, let's start with...

                    NICK
          An '82 Margaux?

                    HEATHER
               (laughing)
          Okay... is it good?

                    NICK
          Good?
               (pause for effect)
          It will make you believe in God.

Heather smiles. It's going to be that type of interview.

INT. IL PECCATORE RESTAURANT - LATER

The wine is almost all gone and the plates are half empty.

                    NICK
          So what is the focus of your piece?

                    HEATHER
          You.

                    NICK
          You want to know how I live with myself?

                    HEATHER
               (smiling)
          No, I don't imagine that's a problem. I
          want to know how you see yourself.

                    NICK
          I'm a mediator between two sects of
          society that are trying to reach an
          accommodation.

                    HEATHER
          Interesting. My other interviews have
          pinned you as a mass murderer, profiteer,
          pimp, bloodsucker, child killer, and my
          personal favorite, Yuppie Mephistopheles.

                    NICK
          Sounds like a balanced article.

                    HEATHER
          Who else should I talk to?

                    NICK
          Fifty-five million American smokers, for
          starters or perhaps the American tobacco
          farmer who is constantly being treated
          like a drug smuggler.

                    HEATHER
          I actually plan on speaking to a tobacco
          farmer.

                    NICK
          Fine people. Salt of the earth.

                    HEATHER
          Nick. Why do you do this? What motivates
          you?

                    NICK
          You really want to know?

Heather leans in with intrigue. Nick turns off her recorder.

                    NICK (CONT'D)
          Population control.

Heather laughs.

                    HEATHER
          You're bad.

Their eyes meet for a charged beat. Nick relents to her
seduction.

                    NICK
               (shrugs)
          Everyone's got a mortgage to pay.

Nick takes a sip of his wine.

                    NICK (V.O.)
          The Yuppie Nuremberg Defense.

Puts down the wine.

                    NICK (CONT'D)
          I just also happen to have an ex-wife and
          a son in private school.

Heather turns the recorder on.

                    HEATHER
          Is a mortgage really much of a life goal?

                    NICK
          Ninety-nine percent of everything that is
          done in the world, good or bad is done to
          pay a mortgage. Perhaps the world would
          be a better place if everyone rented.

                    HEATHER
          Why don't you rent?

                    NICK
          Oh, I rent as well.

                    HEATHER
          Really?

                    NICK
          My son, his mother, and her boyfriend
          live in my house. I live in my apartment.

                    HEATHER
          And what does Nick Naylor's apartment
          look like?

                    NICK
          Nothing impressive. It wouldn't make the
          real estate section.

                    HEATHER
          Can I see it?

                    NICK
          You want to see my apartment?

                    HEATHER
          I want to see where the devil sleeps.

Heather gives a smile that stops Nick. If we held one more
moment, we'd see him say "check please", but instead we...

                                        CUT TO:

INT. BEDROOM - NICK NAYLOR'S APARTMENT - NIGHT

Wide static shot of the whole room. Somewhere in frame, in
bed, Nick and Heather are doing what could only be described
as... fucking.

However, the sound is faint. Subtle headboard knocking, light
moan and grunt, with just a dash of mattress squeak. Don't
get me wrong, the sex is passionate. We're just uninvolved.

                    NICK (V.O.)
          I have to admit, women find my job...
          really sexy.

INT. KITCHEN - NICK NAYLOR'S APARTMENT - MOMENTS LATER

Similar shot of the kitchen. Static and quiet. At the end of
the island, Nick is fucking Heather against the counter. One
of her legs is up on the stove while she grabs the suspended
pan rack for balance.

                    NICK (V.O.)
          It's kind of this bad boy in a suit thing
          that gets women hot, or so I'm told.

INT. LIVING ROOM - NICK NAYLOR'S APARTMENT - MOMENTS LATER

Similar shot of the living room. Serene. Almost boring. Nick
is fucking Heather against a large window, looking over the
Washington DC skyline.

                    NICK (V.O.)
          I'm sure she finds me charming, but
          somewhere in the back of her head she's
          thinking - half a million people a year.
          Dangerous.

INT. KITCHEN - JILL NAYLOR RESIDENCE - NEXT MORNING

Jill and Joey eat scrambled eggs with orange juice. After a
beat, Joey looks to his mom.

                    JOEY
          Mom, why can't I go to California?

                    JILL
          Because... California is just not a safe
          place, and besides, I'm not sure if it's
          appropriate for your father to bring you
          on a business trip.

                    JOEY
          Appropriate for who?

                    JILL
          What?

                    JOEY
          Mom, is it possible that you're taking
          the frustration of your failed marriage
          out on me?

                    JILL
               (raised eyebrow)
          Excuse me?

                    JOEY
          This California trip seems like a great
          learning opportunity and a chance for me to
          get to know my father. But if you think
          it's more important to use me to channel
          your own frustration against the man you no
          longer love, then I'll understand.

Jill drops her fork as Joey goes back to his eggs.

                                        CUT TO:

EXT. JILL NAYLOR'S RESIDENCE - DAY

Joey gets into a TOWNCAR beside his father.

                    NICK
          How did you convince her?

                    JOEY
          It was an argument, not a negotiation.

JOEY MUSIC BEGINS.

I/E TRAVEL MONTAGE FROM DC TO LA. (VIDEO)

Riding in a cab to the airport. Arriving at the terminal.
Waiting to board. Checking out the cockpit. Playing cards on
the plane. Walking down the aisle towards the bathroom. Nick
doing work on his laptop while Joey does homework.

LA skyline through the window. The plane landing. Waiting for baggage. Getting keys to rental car. Driving up Sepulveda. Seeing things out the car window: Homeless guy with screenplay, a guy selling star maps, actors practicing lines outside a workshop.

EXT. EGO HEADQUARTERS - BEVERLY HILLS - DAY

The Sebring pulls past a SIGN with the agency's logo.

INT. ATRIUM - EGO HEADQUARTERS - DAY

Nick and Joey are sitting on a small modern couch in the center of the giant atrium. They're staring at a GIANT LCD SCREEN that displays the famous National Geographic footage of a Killer Whale decimating a beach of seals, when...

>   JACK (O.C.)
>   Nick?

Nick looks up to find, JACK, an agency assistant with high blood sugar and a nice tan.

>   JACK
>   (all one sentence)
>   Nick! Jack, I'm Jeff's assistant. How was
>   your flight? Jet-lagged? It's like two in
>   DC right now. You really should try
>   Vitamin B, Jeff swears by it. You want an
>   injection?
>   (to Joey)
>   So, who's with you? How are you, dude?
>   What's going on? You guys ever been to LA
>   before?
>   (back to Nick)
>   Wanna head back to Jeff's office? In fact
>   we probably should. He's a punctual
>   being.

Nick and Joey stare back in shock and awe.

INT. CORRIDOR, EGO HEADQUARTERS - DAY

Jack moves confidently through the building. He owns this place. Nick and Joey try to keep up.

>   JACK
>   We originally had some problems with the
>   exterior mirrored glass. The reflection
>   of the sun was causing head-on collisions
>   on Wilshire.

                    NICK
          I hope everyone was alright.

                    JACK
          They got three picture deals at
          Paramount. I think they'll live.

                    NICK
          Well, the building is very nice.

Jack stops briefly.

                    JACK
          Tell Jeff how much you like it. He put a
          lot of himself into this building. And
          you know something. *It shows.*

Jack continues walking. They pass a Japanese man in
traditional farm clothes, raking a rock garden.

                    JACK
              (to Japanese man)
          'Sup Hiroshi?
              (continuing)
          Keep going... that sand's not going to
          rake itself.

EXT. OUTSIDE PATHWAY - EGO HEADQUARTERS - DAY

Jack walks Nick and Joey past a KOI POND.

                    JACK
              (whispering)
          That one over there, seven thousand
          dollars.

                    NICK
          Seven thousand, for a fish?

Jack tosses some FISH FOOD from his pocket. The Koi go crazy.

                    JACK
          Kinda makes you want to stop eating
          sushi, but I guess you kind of have to.
              (pointing to another fish)
          That one over there, swear to you, twelve
          thousand. Gift from Oprah.

                    JOEY
          Do you have any sharks?

                    JACK
          No, we're really, very nice here.

INT. ELEVATOR BANK - EGO HEADQUARTERS - DAY

Jack presses the up button, then points out a SCULPTURE.

                    JACK
          It's a Chamberlain. Office-warming
          present from Matthew McConaughey.

                    NICK
          Generous gift.

                    JACK
              (laughing)
          Yeah, right.
              (suddenly serious)
          Don't get me wrong. Matthew is a
          tremendously talented individual and an
          extremely decent human being. However,
          before Jeff took him on, he was a face.
          Now he's a name.

"Bing" - The elevator arrives.

INT. ELEVATOR, EGO HEADQUARTERS - DAY

Jack rests on one side of the elevator, as Nick and Joey hug
the opposite corner.

                    JACK
          You hear that?

The elevator is completely silent. Not even a hiss. Nick and
Joey shake their heads.

                    NICK
          No...

                    JACK
              (smiles)
          Exactly.

"Bing" - The elevator arrives.

INT. UPSTAIRS CORRIDOR, EGO HEADQUARTERS - DAY

Jack leads Nick and Joey past another assistant's desk.

                    JACK
               (to assistant)
          Hey Neil, I'm going to impale your mom on
          a spike and feed her dead body to my dog
          with syphilis.

The assistant grabs his chest and cracks up.

                    ASSISTANT
          Ah, Jack, you got me.

Jack turns to a stunned Nick and Joey.

                    JACK
          Inside joke.

INT. RECEPTION AREA - EGO HEADQUARTERS - DAY

Jack leads Nick and Joey through the MAJOR DOORS of Jeff's
office into a waiting room.

                    JACK
          As you can see, jeff really loves Asian
          shit.
               (to Joey)
          I'm going to bring your dad in now. Can I
          get you anything while you're waiting?
          Orange Juice? Coffee? Red Bull?

INT. JEFF'S OFFICE - EGO HEADQUARTERS - DAY

Simple. Post modern. The desk is completely clean. Behind it
is a Japanese war mural of pure carnage. Somewhere else in
the room sits a Samurai suit of armor posed in the act of
ritual suicide.

Nick exhales.

                    NICK
          Great office.

                    JACK
          Jeff basically designed the whole thing.
          The architect just made the drawings...

                    JEFF (O.C.)
          ... Stop it Jack. Next you're going to
          tell Nick what position I played for the
          Bruins.

                    JACK
               (half under his breath)
          Cornerback.

JEFF emerges like a magic trick. He is fit, tanned, and
dressed head-to-toe in Italian.

                    JEFF
          Jeff Megal.

                    NICK
          Nick Naylor.

                    JEFF (CONT'D)
               (shaking Nick's hand)
          Mr. Naylor is here to find a way to get
          cigarettes into the hands of someone
          other than the usual RAV's.

                    NICK
          RAV's?

                    JEFF
          Russians, Arabs, and Villains.

                    NICK
          Oh, well, then I guess yes. That is why
          I'm here.

                    JEFF
          Good. I think we can help you.

                    JACK
          Jeff invented product placement.

                    NICK
          I feel I have to ask, are you concerned
          at all with the health element?

They begin to walk towards Jeff's desk.

                    JEFF
          I don't have the answers on that. I'm not
          a doctor. I'm just a facilitator. All I do
          is bring creative people together. What
          information there is, is out there. People
          will decide for themselves. I can't make
          that decision for them. It's not my role.
          It would be morally presumptuous.

Nick is stunned.

                    NICK (V.O.)
          I could learn a lot from this man.

They sit.

                    NICK
          What we need is a smoking role model. A
          real winner.

                    JEFF
          Indiana Jones meets Jerry Maguire...

                    NICK
          ... on two packs a day.

                    JEFF
          But he can't live in contemporary
          society.

                    NICK
          Why not?

                    JEFF
          Health issue is too prevalent. People
          will constantly ask why the character is
          smoking, when it should go unsaid. What
          do you think about the future?

                    NICK
          The future?

                    JEFF
          Yes. After the health thing has blown
          over. A world where smokers and non-
          smokers live in perfect harmony. Sony has
          a futuristic sci-fi picture coming up.
          Message from Sector Six. It all takes
          place on a space station. They're looking
          hard for any type of investor.

                    NICK
          Cigarettes in space?

                    JEFF
          The final frontier, Nick.

                    NICK
          Wouldn't they blow up in an all oxygen
          environment?

                    JEFF
          Easy fix. One line of dialogue... *Thank*
          God we invented the... whatever device.
               (pitches)
          Brad Pitt and Catherine Zeta-Jones have
          just finished ravishing each others bodies
          for the first time. They lay naked,
          suspended mid air, under the heavens. Pitt
          lights up and begins blowing smokes rings
          around every part of Catherine's flawless
          naked body as galaxies go whizzing by above
          the glass dome ceiling. Tell me that
          doesn't work for you?

                    NICK
          I'd see that movie.

                    JEFF
          I'd buy the god damned DVD... y'know if I
          didn't get the free one from the academy.
               (serious again)
          If I were you guys, I'd start on a new
          brand of cigarettes that could be
          released simultaneously to the film.

                    NICK
          Sector Sixes.

                    JEFF
          No one's done that with a cigarette.

                    NICK
          Wow. Where do we go from here?

Jeff gets up and begins walking Nick to the door.

                    JEFF
          You go enjoy the rest of your day with
          your son in Los Angeles, while I find
          answers for our questions.

                    NICK
          Hey, where can I grab a bite around here?

                    JEFF
          Nobu just opened a new place. They only
          serve food that's white.

                    NICK
          Oh.

EXT. ENTRANCE, SANTA MONICA PIER - DUSK

Nick and Joey look up as they step through the GIANT NEON
ARCH at the entrance of the pier. They continue walking.

EXT. CAROUSEL BUILDING, SANTA MONICA PIER - NIGHT

Nick and Joey walk along the famous carousel.

                    JOEY
          So, you go to an office. Then you go on
          TV and talk about cigarettes. Then you
          fly out to LA to talk to some guy who
          works with movie stars. What is that?

                    NICK
          It's my job. I'm a lobbyist.

                    JOEY
          I know, but did you study to do that?

                    NICK
          No, I just kind of figured it out.

                    JOEY
          Then, can't anyone just do that?

                    NICK
          No, I think it requires a moral flexibility
          that kind of goes beyond most people.

                    JOEY
          Do I have flexible morals?

                    NICK
          Well, lets say you became a lawyer, right?
          And, you were asked to defend a murderer.
          Worse than that, a child murderer. The law
          states that every person deserves a fair
          trial. Would you defend him?

                    JOEY
          I don't know. I guess every person
          deserves a fair defense.

                    NICK
          Yeah, well... So do multi-national
          corporations.

EXT. PICNIC TABLES, SANTA MONICA PIER - NIGHT

A mix of LA youth and family sift each way down the pier as
Nick and Joey sit at a table eating hot dogs.

                    JOEY
          So, what happens when you're wrong?

                    NICK
          No, Joey. I'm never wrong.

                    JOEY
          You can't always be right... Right?

                    NICK
          If it's your job to be right. Then,
          you're never wrong.

                    JOEY
               (still confused)
          But, what if you _are_ wrong?

                    NICK
          Okay, lets say you're defending chocolate
          and I'm defending vanilla. Now, if I were
          to say to you, *vanilla is the best flavor
          of ice cream*, you'd say...

                    JOEY
          No, chocolate is.

                    NICK
          Exactly. But you can't win that argument.
          So, I'll ask you: So you think chocolate
          is the end all and be all of ice cream,
          do you?

                    JOEY
               (pushing adamance)
          It's the best ice cream. I wouldn't order
          any other.

                    NICK
          Oh, so it's all chocolate for you, is it?

                    JOEY
          Yes, chocolate is all I need.

                    NICK
          Well, I need more than chocolate. And for
          that matter, I need more than vanilla.
               (MORE)

                    NICK (CONT'D)
          I believe we need freedom and choice when
          it comes to our ice cream and that, Joey
          Naylor. That is the definition of
          liberty.

                    JOEY
          But that's not what we're talking about.

                    NICK
          That's what I'm talking about.

                    JOEY
          But you didn't prove that vanilla was the
          best.

                    NICK
          I didn't have to. I proved that you're
          wrong. And if you're wrong, I'm right.

                    JOEY
          But you still didn't convince me.

                    NICK
          I'm not after you.
              (pointing to the crowded pier)
          I'm after them.

Joey is beginning to understand.

                                                  CUT TO:

EXT. FERRIS WHEEL - NIGHT

Nick and Joey ride to the crest of the Ferris Wheel,
overlooking Santa Monica. They both are enjoying cones of
VANILLA ICE CREAM.

                                                 FADE TO:

INT. NICK'S ROOM, MODERN HOTEL - LATER THAT EVENING

Nick pats Joey on the head, then sends him off to sleep and
closes the separation door between their two rooms.

The telephone rings... Nick answers...

                    NICK
              (checking his watch)
          Hello?

INTERCUT WITH:

INT. JEFF'S OFFICE - EGO HEADQUARTERS - SAME

Jeff stands at the window, now wearing a KIMONO.

> JEFF
> Thought I'd give you a little update.

> NICK
> Oh, hi Jeff. You're still at the office?

> JEFF
> Do you know what time it is in Tokyo
> right now?

> NICK
> No.

> JEFF
> Four PM, tomorrow. It's the future, Nick.

Nick simply mouths the words, *"fuck me"*.

> JEFF
> Anyhow, for Pitt to smoke it's ten
> million. For the pair, it's twenty five.

> NICK
> Twenty five? Usually when I buy two of
> something, I get a discount. What's the
> extra five for?

> JEFF
> Synergy. These are not dumb people. They
> got it right away. Pitt and Zeta-Jones
> lighting up after some cosmic fucking in
> the bubble suite is going to sell a lot
> of cigarettes.

> NICK
> For this kind of money, my people will
> expect some very serious smoking. Can
> Brad Pitt blow smoke rings?

> JEFF
> I don't have that information.

> NICK
> Well, for twenty five million, we'd want
> smoke rings.

                        JEFF
          Oh, there's one more thing. You'd be co-
          financing this picture with the Sultan of
          Glutan. Is that going to be all right?

                        NICK
          The Sultan of Glutan? The one who
          massacred and enslaved his own people?
          Aren't they calling him the "Hitler of
          the South Pacific"?

                        JEFF
          I can't speak to that. I can say that in
          all my dealings with him, he's been a
          very reasonable and sensitive individual.

                        NICK
          I better run it by my people.

                        JEFF
          Of course... Gotta run Nick. London's
          calling. Eight AM in the old empire.

                        NICK
                    (dumbfounded)
          Jeff, when do you sleep?

                        JEFF
          Sunday.

EXT. SANTA MONICA PIER - NIGHT

A wide shot of the pier, lit up at night. One blinking light
stands out in particular. It stays as we...

                                        DISSOLVE TO:

INT. NICK'S HOTEL ROOM - MODERN HOTEL - MORNING

The blinking light is in fact, the message light on Nick's
hotel bedside phone. Nick notices the light, picks up the
receiver, and dials the front desk.

                        NICK
          Yeah, my light is blinking...
                    (listens)
          Oh, okay, send it up.

INT. NICK'S HOTEL ROOM - MODERN HOTEL - MORNING

Nick is sitting on the bed, phone receiver to his ear, with an open BRIEFCASE before him. His expression really makes us want to know what's inside.

> NICK
> (into receiver)
> Captain, I'm sitting in front of an open briefcase...

We pull around the OPEN BRIEFCASE. Inside are stacks of hundred dollar bills, drug-dealer style.

> NICK (CONT'D)
> I don't suppose this is a raise.

Nick picks up a CASH BUNDLE, examining it.

INTERCUT WITH:

EXT. PATIO - THE TOBACCO CLUB - DAY

The captain sits on an outdoor chair. A waiter delivers a mint julep to his side table.

> CAPTAIN
> Nick, you know who Lorne Lutch is?

> NICK
> Of course. He was the Tumbleweed Man. He's dying. He was on Sally last week. Not exactly our biggest fan.

> CAPTAIN
> The money is for him. He has a ranch out there in California. I want you to bring it to him.

> NICK
> He's a cowboy sir. Cowboys don't like bribes.

> CAPTAIN
> It's not a bribe. You're going out there on wings of angels, son.

> NICK
> You mean we're just giving him the money?

>   CAPTAIN
>   I think Christ himself would say, 'That's
>   mighty white of you, boys.'
>
>   NICK
>   No gag agreement?
>
>   CAPTAIN
>   Hopefully, he'll be so damn overcome with
>   gratitude, he'll <u>have</u> to shut up.

INT. JOEY'S ROOM - MODERN HOTEL - DAY

Joey is jumping on the bed.

Nick enters the room, dragging his feet.

>   NICK
>   Hey, kiddo. Look, I've got to go and do a
>   little more work this afternoon.
>
>   JOEY
>   I want to come.

Nick looks into his son's eyes.

EXT. COUNTRY ROAD - DAY

Nick's rented CHRYSLER SEBRING kicks up dust as it cuts by
various ranches.

INT. CHRYSLER SEBRING - DAY

Nick looks over to the passenger seat, where his son stares
out the window, excited. Then Nick turns to the backseat,
where the briefcase sits like an anchor.

EXT. LORNE LUTCH'S RANCH - DAY

Southern style. Broken down. Oxygen tanks on the porch.

Nick pulls up in the front yard. He takes one look at the
house and removes his tie. He gets out of the car, pulls out
the briefcase, and steps forward.

Nick stares at the house, thinking of what condition Lorne
Lutch will be in. He takes in a deep breath and starts towards
the porch. A few steps later, the screen door swings open, and
out of the darkness comes the *"chu-chink"* of a shotgun.

Nick freezes again.

STILLS

Aaron Eckhart, *Nick Naylor*   (All photos by Dale Robinette)

William H. Macy, *Senator Ortolan Finistirre*

Maria Bello, *Polly Bailey*

David Koechner, *Bobby Jay Bliss*

Maria Bello, David Koechner, and Aaron Eckhart

William H. Macy

Cameron Bright, *Joey Naylor,* and Aaron Eckhart

Cameron Bright and Aaron Eckhart

Aaron Eckhart

Aaron Eckhart and Jason Reitman

Director/Writer Jason Reitman on the set

                    LORNE LUTCH
                 (in shadows)
          What the fuck are you doing here?

                    NICK
          Do you... could I... do you have a
          minute?

Lorne emerges from the shadows, rifle in his hands. He's
broad and weathered. A cowboy with lung cancer.

                    LORNE LUTCH
          What do you want?

The Sebring's passenger door flies open and Joey runs out.

                    JOEY
          Dad...

                    NICK
          Joey, get back in the car.

Joey freezes. Nick raises his arms.

                    NICK
          I just want to talk.

A fly buzzes around Nick. Lorne stares him down, then looks
over at Joey who is hyperventilating.

                    LORNE LUTCH
          All right. Come in.

Lorne turns back inside, holding the door open with the
muzzle of his shotgun.

Nick lowers his arms and walks up to the house. Joey stays a
moment, then follows.

INT. LIVING ROOM - LORNE LUTCH'S RANCH HOUSE- DAY

Hot and dusty. Perhaps, a Deer Head. Photos of Lorne with
celebrities and politicians that cease circa 1970.

Lorne returns the shotgun to its rack.

                    LORNE LUTCH
          Pearl, we've got company.

PEARL, Lorne's wife, nurse, and reason to be alive enters the
room from a hallway and freezes at the sight of Nick.

                    PEARL
          Mister, you've got a lot'a'nerve...

                    LORNE LUTCH
               (gesturing to Joey)
          Pearl. Show this young man some Ice Tea?

Joey's mind is in hyperdrive, trying to keep up with the
information: *Who is my father?*

Pearl pats Joey on the back and leads him into the kitchen.
However, Joey finds a seat where he can still view the action
in the living room.

Nick takes a seat on the couch, while Lorne eases into his
rocking chair.

                    LORNE LUTCH
          Saw you on... weren't you on that Joan
          show?

                    NICK
          Yeah.

                    LORNE LUTCH
          You're lucky you made it out of there
          alive.

                    NICK
          Tobacco used to be all over television.
          Now, TV is leading the witch hunt.

                    LORNE LUTCH
          Strange business. After I got diagnosed,
          I flew east to attend the annual
          stockholders' meeting. I stood up and
          told them that they ought to limit their
          advertising. And do you know what your
          boss said to me?

Nick knows, but doesn't interrupt.

                    LORNE LUTCH
          He said 'We're certainly sorry to hear
          about your medical problem. However,
          without knowing your medical history, we
          can't comment further.' Then they tried
          to pretend I never worked for them. I
          mean I've got pay stubs, but hell I'm on
          the damn billboards.
               (breaks for breath)
                    (MORE)

                         LORNE LUTCH (CONT'D)
          I never even smoked Tumbleweeds. I smoked
          Kools.

The two men chuckle over this.

                         LORNE LUTCH
          You look like a nice enough fellah. What
          are you doing working for these assholes?

Hold on Nick as he chooses his words carefully.

                         NICK
          I'm good at it. I'm better at doing this
          than I ever was at doing anything else.

                         LORNE LUTCH
          Well hell, son, I was good at shooting
          Koreans, but I didn't make it my career.

There is a pause as Lorne studies Nick.

                         LORNE LUTCH (CONT'D)
          I suppose we all got to pay the mortgage.

Nick exhales.

INT. KITCHEN - LORNE LUTCH'S RANCH HOUSE - SAME

Pearl gives Joey an Ice Tea.

                         PEARL
          Your dad always bring you along like
          this?

                         JOEY
          No, I live with my mom.

                         PEARL
          Did he tell you why he's here today?

                         JOEY
          He said, your husband is the Tumbleweed
          Man.

                         PEARL
          Not anymore.

The PHONE rings. Pearl gets up and turns on the TV. Cartoons.

                         PEARL
          You want any more, just grab it from the
          fridge.

Pearl exits through the back of the kitchen.

As soon as she's gone, Joey scoots up to the doorway
overlooking the living room.

INT. LIVING ROOM - LORNE LUTCH'S RANCH HOUSE - SAME

Lorne gets down to business.

> LORNE LUTCH (CONT'D)
> So, you here to talk me into shutting up?
> Is that what's in that case of yours?

Joey stares, trying to keep up with the action.

> NICK
> Yeah, basically...
>   (picking up the briefcase)
> No, not basically. That's exactly it.

> LORNE LUTCH
> My dignity ain't for sale.

> NICK
> This isn't an offer. It's a gift. The
> taxes have all been paid. You get to keep
> it no matter what you do. The idea is
> that somehow your guilt will prevent you
> from bad-mouthing us.

> LORNE LUTCH
> Were you supposed to tell me all that?

> NICK
> No. Just apologize, give you the money,
> and leave.

> LORNE LUTCH
> Then why are you telling me this?

A moment. Joey gets closer. Then...

Nick ignites. He looks up at Lorne.

> NICK
> Because this way, you'll take the money.

> LORNE LUTCH
> Why would I do that?

                    NICK
          Because you're mad.

                    LORNE LUTCH
          Damn straight.

                    NICK
          The first thing you'll do is call the LA
          Times and CNN.

                    LORNE LUTCH
          Uh huh.

                    NICK
          And insist on Bonnie Carlton. She does
          really good controlled outrage. Tell them
          no Bonnie, no story, watch it on MSNBC.

                    LORNE LUTCH
               (trying to keep up)
          Okay...

                    NICK
          When they get here, open up the case and
          dump all the cash out onto the floor.

                    LORNE LUTCH
          Why?

Nick is really cooking now. He gets up...

                    NICK
          Trust me, it'll look more effective.
          Here, look...

Nick opens the briefcase and begins to dump the MONEY onto
the floor... it's a lot of money.

Joey's eyes widen.

                    NICK
               (shaking the case)
          And don't forget to shake every last
          bundle out. And if you can, you know,
          give a cough or two.

Nick dumps the briefcase.

                    NICK (CONT'D)
          Once it's all out, you tell them what
          you're going to do with it.

                    LORNE LUTCH
                 (now standing)
          What am I going to do with it?

                    NICK
          Donate it. Start the Lorne Lutch Cancer
          Foundation. You'll have a ranch and a
          fair and a 5K...
                 (aside to Lorne)
          The 5K is a must.
                 (back to pitch)
          The TV coverage will be great...

                    LORNE LUTCH
          Wait, what about my family?

                    NICK
          Whoa, Lorne, you can't keep the money.

                    LORNE LUTCH
                 (caught in the enthusiasm)
          Why the hell not?

                    NICK
          What, denounce us and then keep the blood
          money? I mean, look at it.

Lorne looks at the pile of money. One million dollars is a
lot of money.

                    LORNE LUTCH
          I've got to think it over.

                    NICK
          You can't denounce us next week, Lorne.
          News doesn't work that way.

                    LORNE LUTCH
          I don't suppose I can denounce you for
          half of it.

                    NICK
          No Lorne. You either keep all the money
          or give it all away.

Lorne looks to Nick for support. Nick has now turned off.
Lorne looks back down at the money.

INT. CHRYSLER SEBRING - DAY

Nick drives. Joey looks to his father with pride. The
briefcase is nowhere in sight.

> JOEY
> Dad, how did you know he was going to
> take the money?

Nick shoots a look at Joey, ready to question how he saw
Lorne and the briefcase, but relents - *He saw.*

> NICK
> You'd have to be crazy to turn down all
> that money. As soon as I saw he wasn't
> crazy, I knew he'd take it.

> JOEY
> Would you have taken it?

> NICK
> If I were him?
> (thinks for a second)
> Sure.

Joey thinks for a second.

> JOEY
> So would I.

Nick pats his son's head while Joey enjoys the warm glow of
his father's affection.

> CUT TO:

AN OUT OF FOCUS GRID...

As it comes into focus, we recognize it as a collection of
slides from a photo shoot of Nick.

INT. HEATHER HOLLOWAY'S OFFICE, WASHINGTON PROBE - DAY

Heather Holloway bends over a light box, using a LOOP. She
moves from one slide to another, judging them. She stops on
a perfect shot. Smiles. Looks around for a beat, then puts it
in her shirt pocket.

As Heather walks away, we begin to hear...

                    RON GOODE (O.C.)
          He's an animal, sir. You can't take your
          guard down for a second.

INT. CORRIDOR, CNBC STUDIOS - NIGHT

RON GOODE is walking Senator FINISTIRRE towards an INTERVIEW
CHAIR in front of a studio camera. A small crew awaits them.

                    FINISTIRRE
               (pulling off make-up bib)
          Ron, shut up...
               (sits in the chair)
          I've tangoed with presidents, Arabs, and
          Indian chiefs. I think I can handle Mr.
          Nick Naylor.

We pull around Finistirre's shoulder to reveal a MONITOR. On
which, DENNIS MILLER is getting final touch ups.

                    FINISTIRRE (CONT'D)
          Hello, Dennis.

                                                  CUT TO:

INT. THE DENNIS MILLER SHOW - MOMENTS LATER

DENNIS MILLER sits confidently at his desk.

                    DENNIS
          Alright, welcome back kids. We have two
          guests on our show tonight. First,
          joining us from our Washington studio. He
          is the Democratic Senator from Vermont -
          Please welcome Ortolan Finistirre.
          Welcome Senator.

The IMAGE of Finistirre sitting in the DC studio appears in
split screen next to Dennis.

                    FINISTIRRE
               (smiling)
          Good to be here, Dennis.

                    DENNIS
          And joining us in our Los Angeles studio.
          He is the chief spokesperson for the
          Academy of Tobacco Studies - Nick Naylor.
          Nick, Welcome.

Widen to reveal Nick sitting across from Dennis.

                    NICK
Pleasure to be here.

                    DENNIS
Alright, I understand you went on the
Joan Lunden Show recently. Didn't make a
lot of friends over there, did you.

                    NICK
I will say that I don't think I'll be
getting my annual invitation to the
Finistirre Labor Day Barbecue.

                    FINISTIRRE
Well, I continue to offer an open
invitation to Mr. Naylor to join us in
Congress to discuss the inclusion of our
new poison label, which if I might say...

                    DENNIS
Nick - Ready to trek up the hill and
testify before Congress?

                    NICK
Not as long as the Senator is calling for
me to be fired. It's not exactly a
welcome invitation.

                    DENNIS
Bit of a mixed message, Senator.

                    FINISTIRRE
Not as mixed as Big Tobacco's stance on
the dangers of smoking cigarettes.

Nick begins to laugh, taking Dennis and Finistirre off guard.

                    DENNIS
Now, what are you laughing at? You're a
wind-up artist. Give the man his due. He's
got a bit of a point there, doesn't he?

                    NICK
I just can't help myself, Dennis. I'm
tickled by the idea of the gentleman from
Vermont calling me a hypocrite. This from a
man, who in one day, held a press
conference where he called for the American
tobacco fields to be "slashed and burned".
Then, he jumped on a private jet.
                    (MORE)

                    NICK (CONT'D)
Flew down to Farm Aid and road a tractor on
stage as he bemoaned the downfall of the
American farmer. It just makes me laugh.

Joey's smile says: *My dad is one bad ass motherfucker.*

                    DENNIS
Care to comment, Senator?

                    FINISTIRRE
        (straining)
I - Um - No.

                    DENNIS
Eloquent in its brevity.
        (switches gears)
Emotional issue. Lets take some calls.
Herndon, Virginia, you're on the show.

                    CALLER
Dennis, has anyone ever announced that
they're going to kill someone live on
your show?

Dennis thinks the man is kidding and quips back...

                    DENNIS
My demo's been called quirky, but no, at
this point we're not skewing to the
emotionally unstable.

                    CALLER
Then it's your lucky day, because I'm
here to tell you that within a week,
we're going to dispatch Mr. Naylor from
this planet, for all the pain and
suffering he's caused the world.

The phone clicks. An awkward pause. Nick is stunned.

Joey is suddenly very scared.

An uncomfortable pause. Then...

                    DENNIS
As I said, emotional issue.
        (looks around)
We're going to break now. I've got to
fire a call screener.

EXT. JILL NAYLOR'S HOUSE - EVENING

Nick watches from the backseat of a TOWNCAR as Joey runs
right by his mom into the house. Jill meanwhile stares back
at Nick and shakes her head. She evidently saw the show.

INT. UNKNOWN APARTMENT CORRIDOR - EVENING

The FRONT DOOR swings open revealing Nick. A woman's hand
comes into frame and strokes his face. She then comes into
frame herself and embraces him, revealing her to be HEATHER.

INT. HEATHER'S BEDROOM - NIGHT

Nick is lying on Heather's bed, with his head at the foot of
the bed. The TV is on behind him. Suddenly, Heather leaps up
onto the bed, startling Nick. She straddles him, wearing his
dress shirt and tie... and begins to do his impersonation...

                    HEATHER
                (being Nick)
          Kids... don't do drugs... smoke
          cigarettes...

Heather attempts a "Nick Naylor smile", then breaks up
giggling.

                    NICK
          That's great. Really, I feel like I'm
          looking into a mirror.

Heather continues as Nick, pantomiming a tape recorder.

                    HEATHER
                (mock brainstorming)
          New idea... Cigarettes for the
          homeless... We'll call them Hobo's.

                    NICK
          Okay, now that's awful.

                    HEATHER
          Any better than Sector Sixes?

Nick smiles uncomfortably. He obviously divulged this in the
heat of passion...

                    NICK
                (trying to laugh it off)
          Right...

Heather bolts upright...

                    NICK
          Oh my god... you're on TV!

ON TV: A NEWS ANCHOR SPEAKS ON MUTE

A photo of NICK on the Dennis Miller show pops up over the
anchor's shoulder. The caption reads LOBBYIST ON THE LOOKOUT.

                    NICK
               (reading caption)
          Lobbyist on the lookout? Are you kidding
          me?

Heather reaches under the blanket to pull off Nick's pants.

                    HEATHER
          I wanna fuck you while I watch you on TV.

                    NICK
          And they call me sick.

                    HEATHER
          Hurry, I don't want to miss your clip...

She giggles.

                    NICK
          Um, okay.

                    HEATHER
          Tell me more about Los Angeles.

                    NICK
          Huh?

Nick gives a questioning look, when she does something with
her hips that makes Nick smile as his eyes go to half mast.

                                        FADE TO:

INT. BERT'S RESTAURANT - DAY

The MOD Squad at their regular table.

                    NICK
          ... He says *he wants to trail me*
          everywhere. I say *who's paying for it*. He
          says *the tobacco company*.
               (MORE)

              NICK (CONT'D)
So I say to him, *I don't need body guards. I'm a man of the people.*

              BOBBY JAY
Rock on, Kennedy.

              POLLY
We're all going to need bodyguards soon enough. Did you see the coverage the fetal-alcohol people got themselves over this weekend. They made it sound like we encourage pregnant mothers to drink. I'm surprised *I* didn't get kidnapped on the way to work this morning.

This catches Nick's attention.

              NICK
              (patronizing)
I don't think people who work for the alcoholic beverage industry have to worry about being kidnapped, just yet.

All movement stops. Polly stares Nick down.

              POLLY
Pardon me?

              NICK
Look, nothing personal, but tobacco generates a little more heat than alcohol.

              POLLY
Oh, this is news.

              NICK
My product puts away 475 thousand a year...

              POLLY
              (rhetorical)
Oh, now 475 is a legit number?

              NICK
Okay, 435 thousand, that's twelve hundred a day. How many alcohol related deaths a year? A hundred thousand, tops? Two hundred seventy something a day? Well wow-wee. Two hundred and seventy people. Oh, the tragedy.
              (MORE)

                    NICK (CONT'D)
          Excuse me if I don't exactly see
          terrorists getting excited enough to
          kidnap anyone from the alcohol industry.

                    BOBBY JAY
          Okay, let's breathe.

                    NICK
          How many gun deaths a year in the US,
          Bobby Jay?

                    BOBBY JAY
          Eleven thousand.

                    NICK
          Eleven thousand? You've got to be kidding
          me? Thirty a day. That's less than
          passenger car mortalities. No terrorist
          would bother with either of you.

Nick goes back to his food. A long silence follows.

Nick realizes that he's shoved a little too hard.

                    NICK
          Look, this is a stupid argument.

                    POLLY
          I'll say.

                    NICK
          I'm sure both of you warrant vigilante
          justice.

                    POLLY
          Thank you.

EXT. SIDE STREET - WASHINGTON DC - DAY

Nick walks away from Bert's. He goes to get in his BMW, when
a VAN screeches to a halt beside him.

Nick looks up, but it's too late. The VAN DOOR slides open
and he is yanked into the opening as the wheels peel out.

INT. KIDNAPPER'S MINI-VAN - DAY

Nick is immediately tackled to the ground by two hooded men.
The two men BLINDFOLD Nick, then HANDCUFF him with zip chord.

                    NICK
          Wait... huh... you got the wrong guy!
          Please, stop! Who are you guys?!

No answer.

EXT. WASHINGTON DC STREET - DAY

The Kidnapper's MINI-VAN flies by.

EXT. ST. EUTHANASIUS - DAY

Pushing in on the classroom building.

INT. JOEY'S CLASSROOM - NEXT DAY

It's speech day. A FLIGHTY GIRL who, one day, will never
graduate Vidal Sassoon's hair academy no matter how hard she
tries is making her finishing remarks.

                    FLIGHTY GIRL
          ... and freedom means that we can do what
          we want and that's really important
          because otherwise we couldn't be free and
          that's why America is the best government
          in the world.

INT. KIDNAPPER VAN - SAME

The two men proceed to swiftly cut off Nick's clothes with
scissors.

                    NICK
          Wo, wo, wo!... Can we get a dialogue
          going here?

A voice breaks the silence. A friendly voice, actually.
Saturday morning cartoon friendly. It could be Mr. Rogers.

                    KIDNAPPER
          Nick, we want you to stop killing people.
          So many people. Half a million people a
          year in the U.S.

                    NICK
          There's no data to support that.

                    KIDNAPPER
          Nick... you're not on TV anymore.

INT. JOEY'S CLASSROOM

Joey's TEACHER wakes the class up with a heavy cupped-hand applause. The rest of the class follows suit, half awake.

                    TEACHER
          Okay, Joey, it's you're turn.

Joey stays seated for a moment and takes in a deep breath like his father usually does.

INT. KIDNAPPER'S MINI-VAN - DAY

The two men in hoods pull out cardboard BOXES. From the boxes they pull little PACKAGES.

                    KIDNAPPER
          Nick, how much do you smoke a day?

One man pulls out something white, then SLAPS it down on Nick's CHEST, where it sticks like a band-aid. Then the other man does the same. The two men start covering Nick's entire body with these little white stickers...

SLAP!... SLAP!... SLAP!, SLAP!... SLAP!

                    NICK
          What are you doing?

                    KIDNAPPER
          According to the box, each one of those
          patches contains twenty-one milligrams of
          nicotine. That's like what? One Pack?

SLAP!... SLAP!, SLAP!

                    NICK
          Look, Our industry has been working hand
          in hand...

                    KIDNAPPER
          Nick, just listen, all right?

INT. JOEY'S CLASSROOM - SAME

Joey stands in front of the class. He takes a deep breath.

                    JOEY
          What makes America the best government? A
          passion that doesn't exist anywhere else
          in the world?

INT. KIDNAPPER VAN - SAME

                    KIDNAPPER
          Says here there are many adverse
          reactions from these things. Let's see,
          Erythema, constipation, dyspepsia,
          nausea, myalgia...

                    NICK
          My industry does forty-eight billion a
          year in revenue.

SLAP!, SLAP!...SLAP!

                    KIDNAPPER
               (continues reading)
          Pharyngitis, Sinusitis,...

INT. JOEY'S CLASSROOM - SAME

Joey builds with confidence.

                    JOEY
          ... Sure you can call it capitalism. A
          free market... A celebration of tariff
          breakdowns?

INT. KIDNAPPER VAN - SAME

                    KIDNAPPER
               (struggles with word)
          Dys-men-or-rhea. I don't even want to
          know what that means.

Nick is starting to struggle.

                    NICK
          I would guess that you could start by
          asking for five million and work your way
          up from there.

SLAP!, SLAP!

                    KIDNAPPER
          But I don't want any money, Nick.

                    NICK
          Well, what do you want? I mean, I'm all
          ears, here.

INT. JOEY'S CLASSROOM - SAME

We push into Joey.

> JOEY
> I have another word for it. Love.

INT. KIDNAPPER VAN - SAME

SLAP!... SLAP!

> KIDNAPPER
> Nick... what does any man want? The love
> of a woman? Crisp bacon? An average life
> span over eighty years?

The slapping stops. Nick begins to hyperventilate.

INT. JOEY'S CLASSROOM - DAY

We see Joey taking in the applause of his classmates.

INT. KIDNAPPER VAN - DAY

Nick struggles for air and begins to turn red.

> KIDNAPPER (CONT'D)
> Oh, Nick. You don't look so good...

FADE TO WHITE:

INT. HOTEL CORRIDOR - DAY - VIDEO FOOTAGE DREAM SEQUENCE

Bad Grainy Yellow Video and Kenny G - We're watching the
HOTEL CHANNEL where they instruct you how to escape a fire.

Smoke fills the ceiling of the corridor.

Smoke curls under the door.

> NARRATOR
> (comforting female)
> *If you see or smell smoke,*

Nick enters the bathroom. As it turns out, he is the subject
of the video.

> NARRATOR
> *Take a wash cloth, soak it with water,*
> *and cover your nose and mouth.*

Nick takes a wash cloth and follows the instructions.

Nick approaches the hotel room door.

>   NARRATOR
> *Before opening your door, check for heat.*

Nick touches the door. He's satisfied. He opens the door and walks into the corridor. People run by. The Fire alarm begins to fade up from the background, getting louder and louder.

>   NARRATOR
> *Do not remove your washcloth. Try at all*
> *times to avoid breathing in the smoke...*

The smoke cloud lowers. The alarm gets louder.

>   NARRATOR
> *If necessary, crawl on your hands and*
> *knees to avoid smoke inhalation.*

Nick takes to all fours, still trying to keep the wash cloth on his face. The alarm gets even louder.

>   NARRATOR
> *If you do happen to inhale the smoke, do*
> *not be alarmed. There are still no*
> *conclusive studies that link the*
> *inhalation of smoke to emphysema.*

Nick looks up confused dropping his wash cloth. He stands up in the smoke just as we...

>   SLAM CUT TO:

INT. NICK'S RECOVERY ROOM - ST. JOSEPH'S HOSPITAL - DAY

Nick opens his eyes. Next to him, a NURSE is fiddling with Nick's various monitors, whose beeps match the dream.

The nurse catches Nick out of the corner of her eye...

>   NURSE
> You woke up.

>   NICK (V.O.)
> Perhaps a bad choice of inflection? Is
> she implying that I could have just as
> easily, not?

Without waiting a beat, the nurse grabs the BED REMOTE and presses the up button, lifting Nick into the seated position.

Waiting before him is a line of familiar people. As the Romper Room lady would say, *I see...*

BOBBY JAY, POLLY, JOEY, GIZELLE, BR, a DOCTOR, the NURSES, and right in the middle is a BIG SCREEN TV, on which is a live image of the CAPTAIN in his own hospital bed. They all just stare silently, then Joey runs up and hugs his dad.

>   JOEY
>   I was so scared.

Nick embraces his son.

>   NICK
>   Hey Joey. What happened?

The doctor breaks from the group, and takes to Nick's side.

>   DOCTOR
>   No non-smoker could ever have withstood
>   the amount of nicotine you had in your
>   bloodstream.
>   (flustered)
>   I hate to say it, but... cigarettes saved
>   your life.

>   NICK
>   Can I quote you on that?

>   CAPTAIN
>   (on TV)
>   You're a real trooper, my boy.

>   NICK
>   Captain, where are you?

>   CAPTAIN
>   (on TV)
>   Winston-Salem General... Damned heart
>   failed on me again. Thought we could be
>   room mates.

>   DOCTOR
>   Uh, Nick, before we get side tracked,
>   there is one thing.

>   NICK
>   Don't get all dramatic on me, doc.

>   DOCTOR
>   You can't smoke.
>
>   NICK
>   No problem. I've quit before. I did
>   during the pregnancy. How long, you
>   think?
>
>   DOCTOR
>   I don't think you understand. It's a
>   miracle that you came out of this alive.
>   Any smoking... one cigarette could put
>   you back into a paralytic state. Your
>   body just can't handle it.

Nick looks around the room. It is evident from everybody's
expressions that they already knew this.

>   BR
>   Nick, I don't want to put any more
>   pressure on you, but there's a camera
>   crew standing by. If we want to make the
>   evening news...

Nick looks around the room, then to his nurse.

>   NICK
>   Hey, you want to unhook me here.

>   CUT TO:

INT. NICK'S HOSPITAL ROOM - LATER (TV INTERVIEW)

The room is now lit by TV lights. Nick is being interviewed
in bed. Joey sits by his side.

>   NICK
>   Well, this just goes to prove what I've
>   been saying for a long time: These
>   nicotine patches are just deadly.
>   Smoking... saved my life.
>
>   INTERVIEWER
>   Considering your condition, will you
>   still be able to appear before Senator
>   Finistirre's sub-committee hearing on the
>   usage of poison labels on cigarette
>   packaging?

                    NICK
          I think now more than ever, it is
          imperative that I be present. Nothing
          will keep me from testifying.

We pull out from the image, revealing we are in...

INT. SENATOR FINISTIRRE'S OFFICE - DAY

FINISTIRRE and RON Goode from the Joan show watch in pain.

                    FINISTIRRE
          Fucking kidnapping.

Ron turns off the TV.

                    RON GOODE
          I don't understand, sir. Aren't we
          considering the kidnapping a good thing?

                    FINISTIRRE
          Well, he didn't die.

                    RON GOODE
          He was almost killed, sir.

                    FINISTIRRE
          That's the point. Now he looks like a
          victim. Lucky bastard.

Ron doesn't quite know how to respond.

INT. CAFETERIA - ST. JOSEPH'S HOSPITAL - DAY

Joey joins the MOD squad in their similar eating positions.
Only, now Bert's Restaurant has been replaced by the St.
Joseph's Hospital Commissary.

                    BOBBY JAY
          The way I heard it, DC police found you
          naked, lying in Lincoln's crotch...

FLASH IMAGE: Nick. Naked. Covered in nicotine patches.
Sprawled across Lincoln's giant marble lap ala Pieta.

                    BOBBY JAY (CONT'D)
          ... covered in nicotine patches, with a
          sign over your head that said...

                    POLLY
          Stop it, he doesn't need the details.

                    BOBBY JAY
          It was some pretty fucked up shit...

                    POLLY
               (to Bobby Jay)
          Shhh...
               (to Nick)
          How do you feel?

                    NICK
          I don't know. For the first time, I'm
          thinking these cigarettes are pretty
          dangerous.

                    BOBBY JAY
          You might be right about that.

Polly smiles. Meanwhile, Bobby Jay reaches into his inner
Vest pocket, pulls out a small PISTOL, and begins to hide it
in Nick's wheel chair.

                    POLLY
          What are you doing?

                    BOBBY JAY
          I know it looks small, but it really does
          the trick. One shot, Bam.

                    POLLY
          Nick is not shooting anybody.

                    JOEY
               (re: gun)
          Cool...

                    BOBBY JAY
               (proud)
          Yeah, huh...?

Nick and Polly frown.

                    BOBBY JAY (CONT'D)
               (suddenly restrained)
          ... I mean, guns must be treated with
          respect. Understand?

                    NICK
               (to Bobby Jay)
          You're going to make a great father.

EXT. ACADEMY OF TOBACCO STUDIES - DAY

The trees are noticeable bare.

INT. ACADEMY OF TOBACCO STUDIES - RECEPTION - DAY

The entire Spin Control erupts as Nick enters the front
doors. BR steps forward and raises Nick's arm into the air.
They cheer again.

>   TRAINEE
>   Welcome back!

INT. NICK'S OFFICE - ACADEMY OF TOBACCO STUDIES - DAY

Nick looks pretty weathered, sitting on his sofa. BR enters
for a private chat now that the fanfare has died down.

>   BR
>   You okay?

>   NICK
>   I'm functioning.

>   BR
>   (excited)
>   Good, cause you're booked on all the
>   Sunday talk shows. For once, sympathy is
>   in our corner. We can have our own
>   celebrity victim tour.

>   NICK
>   (not encouraged)
>   Great.

>   BR
>   (more excited)
>   I mean, we couldn't have planned this
>   better ourselves.

>   NICK
>   Maybe next time I can lose a lung.

BR points at Nick as if to say, *not a bad idea.* He begins to
leave, then stops for something.

>   BR
>   Oh, I heard the Heather Holloway article
>   is coming out tomorrow.

                    NICK
               (genuinely surprised)
          Really?

                    BR
          Anything I should be worried about?

                    NICK
          Yes. The Cancer Association. Apparently,
          they have it in for us.

                    BR
          Fuckers.

BR nods and leaves.

INT. BERT'S RESTAURANT - DAY

The MOD squad sits but does not eat. Nick notices.

                    NICK
          What?

                    BOBBY JAY
          I got a call from the paper.

                    NICK
          Really. What did they want?

                    BOBBY JAY
          They wanted to check the spelling of my
          name and job title.

                    POLLY
          You didn't tell her about us did you?

                    NICK
          No, I mean, if anything, in passing.

                    POLLY
          In passing?

                    BOBBY JAY
          Oh god, he fucked her.
               (to Nick)
          I tried to warn you.

                    POLLY
          He didn't fuck her.
               (to Nick)
          You didn't fuck her, did you?

Nick doesn't answer. Polly is beside herself.

>   POLLY
>   When?

>   BOBBY JAY
>   In passing.

>   NICK
>   Look, she's really a nice girl.

>   BOBBY JAY
>   Oh god, we're <u>really</u> fucked.

EXT. JILL'S HOUSE - THE NEXT MORNING

Brad steps out in a BATHROBE. He walks to the bottom of the driveway and picks up the morning paper. Front page reads:

NICK NAYLOR'S SMOKESCREEN

I do it for the mortgage!

Brad shakes his head and sighs.

INT. DC METRO - MORNING

People wait for the subway. Many are reading the PAPER.

>   NICK (V.O.)
>   *Nick Naylor, lead spokesman for big*
>   *tobacco, would have you believe he thinks*
>   *cigarettes are harmless...*

INT. COFFEE SHOP - MORNING

People drink coffee, eat pastries, and read the PAPER.

>   NICK (V.O.)
>   *But really, he's doing it for the*
>   *mortgage...*

INT. BERT'S RESTAURANT - DAY

Push in on Bobby Jay and Polly sit in silence, each reading their own copy of the PAPER. Pan to Polly...

                    POLLY (V.O.)
          The MOD squad, meaning of course
          Merchants-Of-Death is comprised of Polly
          Bailey of the Moderation Council and
          Bobby Jay Bliss of the gun business's own
          advisory group, SAFETY...

Pan to Bobby Jay...

                    BOBBY JAY (V.O.)
          As explained by Naylor, the sole purpose of
          their meetings is to compete for the highest
          death toll as they compare strategies on how
          to dupe the American people.

Bobby Jay and Polly look up at each other in disbelief.

INT. JEFF MEGALL'S OFFICE, EGO HEADQUARTERS - DAY

Jeff is handed a crisp copy of the article with hi-lighted
sections. He immediately devours it...

                    JEFF (V.O.)
          The film, Message from Sector Six would
          emphasize the sex appeal of cigarettes,
          in a way only floating nude copulating
          hollywood stars could...

INT. INTERNET CAFE - DAY

Students at computer terminals, read the article on the
Washington Probe Website.

INT. LORNE LUTCH'S RANCH - DAY

Lorne's FAX machine, albeit an ancient one, spits out the
curled transmission. He reads:

                    LORNE (V.O.)
          This did not stop Nick from bribing the
          dying man with a suitcase of cash to keep
          quiet on the subject of his recent lung
          cancer diagnosis...

INT. KITCHEN - JILL NAYLOR'S RESIDENCE - DAY

Joey runs into room expecting a snack, but instead finds Jill
and Brad hovering over the PAPER.

                    JILL (V.O.)
*Nick's own son Joey Naylor seems to be
being groomed for the job, as he joins his
father on the majority of his trips...*

INT. NICK'S OFFICE - ACADEMY OF TOBACCO STUDIES - DAY

Nick sits at his desk. He is a mess. He taps an unopened copy
of the PAPER, when the intercom suddenly breaks the moment...

                    GIZELLE
                (intercom)
        I have Heather Holloway on line one.

Nick leaps for the phone.

                    NICK
        Heather.

INTERCUT WITH:

INT. HEATHER HOLLOWAY'S OFFICE - SAME

Heather is as cheery as the first time we met her.

                  HEATHER
        Hey, Nick, what did you think?

Nick chooses every word carefully.

                    NICK
        Heather, there is a lot of information in
        here, that is... off the record.

                  HEATHER
        You never said anything about off the
        record.

                    NICK
        I presumed, anything said while I was
        inside you was *privileged*.

                  HEATHER
        If you wanted to talk on a plane or at a
        movie or over dinner, that would have
        been fine. But you wanted to fuck. That's
        fine by me.

Nick is stunned. Even insulted by this realization.

                NICK
You used me?

              HEATHER
        (still friendly)
Come on Nick. Now we're being children.
We both love our jobs. I'm just a
reporter and you're just a lobbyist.

                NICK
How could you do this to me?

              HEATHER
Oh, Nick. For the mortgage.

INT. BR'S OFFICE - DAY

Nick enters as BR is reading the article.

                BR
  Bitch.

                NICK
  Whore.

BR sets down the paper.

                BR
You should have been more careful, Nick.
You've destroyed all the good will
created by your kidnapping.

                NICK
I'll work up a rebuttal. Heather Holloway
isn't the only reporter in town.

                BR
No, there isn't going to be a rebuttal.

                NICK
What do you mean?

                BR
Don't talk to anyone. We're pulling you
from the congressional hearing.

                NICK
You can't pull me from the hearing. All
you'll be doing is giving credence to her
article. I am ready to testify.

> BR
>
> Nick, half of my job is damage control.
> And today, that consists of distancing
> ourselves from you entirely and letting
> you take the heat on this article.

Nick begins to realize he is being fired.

> BR
>
> Your job relied on your ability to keep
> secrets and spin the truth. I can't
> imagine a way in which you could have
> fucked up more. There is just no way I
> could possibly keep you on staff.

> NICK
>
> And I assume you've already run this by
> the Captain?

> BR
>
> The Captain died this morning.

Nick stops. Everything stops.

INT. BOEING 757 - DAY

Nick looks up and finds the permanently lit NON-SMOKING SIGN.

EXT. CEMETERY - DAY

A large crowd has gathered to see a local hero be buried.
Very formal. All black. No grey.

Nick stands alone in the crowd.

A waiter from the Tobacco Club steps forward and places a MINT
JULEP on the Casket as it is lowered into the ground.

EXT. WASHINGTON DC INTERSECTION - LATE AFTERNOON

Nick is stuck in traffic.

INT. NICK'S APARTMENT - NIGHT

Nick slumps into his apartment. We hear his answering machine.

> ANSWERING MACHINE (O.C.)
> *Mr. Naylor, this is Pete in security at*
> *the Academy.*
> (MORE)

           ANSWERING MACHINE (O.C.) (CONT'D)
Your things are waiting for you at the
information kiosk in the lobby. Look,
just pick'm up by Friday, or we're
supposed to throw'm away.

INT. NICK'S APARTMENT - NEXT MORNING

Nick empties his fridge.

           ANSWERING MACHINE (O.C.)
Nick, Jack in Jeff Megall's office. Jeff
really enjoyed meeting you the other day
and is sorry that you two couldn't find a
project to work on. Drop me a line
whenever you're in town. My e-mail is...

INT. NICK'S APARTMENT - LATER

Nick goes through his mail. He becomes transfixed by a lost
child PAMPHLET, reading: *"Have You Seen Me?"*

           ANSWERING MACHINE (O.C.)
Mr. Naylor, this is Special Agent Johnson
with the FBI. Having not found any leads
in your kidnapping investigation, we will
be handing over the case to local DC
police. Please refer to them in the
future for updates and questions...

INT. NICK'S APARTMENT - LATER

Nick is now upside down on his couch, when there's a "KNOCK".

INT. ENTRYWAY - NICK'S APARTMENT - DAY

Nick steps up to the door.

           NICK
Who is it?

           JILL (O.C.)
It's me, Nick.

           NICK
Oh, Jill, this is a bad time... I'm
trying to find that kung fu spot that
kills a human body instantaneously.

           JILL (O.C.)
Let me in Nick.

                    NICK
               (thinks a beat)
          No.

                    JILL (O.C.)
          I brought someone who needs to talk to you.

Nick exhales, then opens the door. Jill brought Joey.

                    NICK
               (to Joey)
          There's a coke in the fridge.

Joey runs past his father to the kitchen. Jill takes a step
forward, then stops next to Nick.

                    JILL
          So, this Heather Holloway must've been
          pret-ty hot...

Nick goes to argue, then concedes...

                    NICK
          Yeah, she's pretty hot.

                    JILL
          Don't take it so hard. A few flaws can be
          appealing. It makes you human.

                    NICK
               (without flinching)
          Who wants to be human?

                    JILL
          I know one person who still thinks
          you're a god.

Nick looks back towards the kitchen.

                                             CUT TO:

INT. KITCHEN, NICK'S APARTMENT - SAME

Nick and Joey sit at the kitchen table, each slumped on their
elbows, mirroring each other in identical positions.

                    JOEY
          Why did you tell that reporter all your
          secrets?

                    NICK
          You're too young to understand.

                    JOEY
          Mom says it's because you have dependency
          issues and it was just a matter of time
          before you threw it all away on some tramp.

Nick pauses.

                    NICK
          Well, that's one theory.

                    JOEY
          Why are you hiding from everybody?

                    NICK
          It has something to with being
          generally hated right now.

                    JOEY
          But it's your job to be generally hated.

Nick smiles.

                    NICK
          It's more complicated than that.

                    JOEY
          You're just making it more complicated so
          you can feel sorry for yourself.

Nick raises an eyebrow.

                    JOEY (CONT'D)
          Like you always said, "If you want an
          easy job, go work for the Red Cross."
          You're a lobbyist. Your job is to be
          right and you're the best at what you do.
          You're the "Sultan of spin"...

                    NICK
          Sultan of spin?

                    JOEY
               (quickly)
          Mom subscribes to Newsweek.
               (back to his pitch)
          Who cares what the Brads of the world
          think? He's not my dad. You are.

Nick looks into Joey's eyes.

>   NICK (V.O.)
>   And right there, looking into Joey's
>   eyes, it all came back in a rush... Why I
>   do what I do...

Push into Nick as we see him change.

>   NICK (V.O.) (CONT'D)
>   Defending the defenseless...

We see a spark of that confidence we saw in the beginning.

>   NICK (V.O.) (CONT'D)
>   Protecting the disenfranchised
>   corporations that have been abandoned by
>   their very own consumers...

>   CUT TO:

OUTRAGEOUS KODAK MOMENTS OF:

EXT. FORREST - DAY

A LOGGER - about to cut down the last tree in an acre of
stumps. He poses with his chainsaw and smiles to camera.

>   NICK (V.O.)
>   The logger.

INT. SWEAT SHOP - DAY

A SWEAT SHOP FOREMAN smiling with his clipboard as countless
children make shoes in the background.

>   NICK (V.O.)
>   The sweat shop foreman.

EXT. OIL RIG - DAY

An OIL DRILLER and his SON smiling as the drilling mechanism
behind them bores into the Pacific Ocean floor.

>   NICK (V.O.)
>   The oil driller.

INT. SCIENCE LAB - DAY

A LAND MINE DEVELOPER presenting a newly designed land mine
to his underlings. They all look up and smile.

                    NICK (V.O.)
          The land mine developer.

EXT. ARCTIC TUNDRA - DAY

A SEAL PELT TRADER holding a beaten baby seal, looks up and
smiles.

                    NICK (V.O.)
          The baby seal poacher.

                                        CUT TO:

INT. BERT'S RESTAURANT - DAY

The MOD SQUAD is at their booth.

                    POLLY
          Baby seal poacher?

                    BOBBY JAY
          Even I think that's kind of cruel.

                    NICK
          Okay, you're missing the point.

                    POLLY
          I must be, because I thought you were
          apologizing.

                    NICK
          I'm getting to that. Look, you two are
          basically my only friends. The last thing
          I ever wanted to do was hurt either of
          you. I can only imagine...

Bobby Jay cracks a smile. Nick stops in question of the look.

                    NICK
               (to Bobby Jay)
          Why are you smiling?
               (immediately to Polly)
          Why is he smiling?

                    POLLY
          He won a hundred bucks on you.

Nick shoots a further confused look.

                    BOBBY JAY
          I bet Polly that you'd spill the
          beans with that reporter.

                    NICK
          That goes against everything we
          stand for.

                    POLLY
          You ratted us out to some reporter
          with tits.

                    BOBBY JAY
               (correcting)
          Glorious tits.

                    NICK
          Only after you created a betting
          pool, testing my incompetence. If
          anything, I thought we had mutual
          professional courtesy.

                    POLLY
          Do you know the beating I've been
          taking at Moderation?

                    NICK
          I'm sure both of you are probably
          under a lot of scrutiny...

                    POLLY
          You can stop using the plural.

Nick looks to Bobby Jay for an explanation.

                    BOBBY JAY
          The guys at SAFETY actually like
          the name, Merchants of Death.
          They're going to make bumper
          stickers. I'll make sure you get
          one.

A WAITRESS arrives with a piece of APPLE PIE with a SLICE OF
AMERICAN CHEESE melted on top for Bobby Jay.

                    NICK
          That's disgusting.

                    BOBBY JAY
               (mid-bite)
          It's American.

Nick shrugs (point taken).

                    POLLY
          Well, I guess this means you won't be
          appearing at Finistirre's sub-
          committee.

                    NICK
          I was kind of looking forward to it
          too. It's kind of cool in a Jimmy
          Stewart sort of way.

                    BOBBY JAY
          More like an Ollie North sort of way.

                    POLLY
          Finistirre would have torn you a new
          asshole, in a house of parliament, no
          less.

                    NICK
          Oh, please. I could have taken him.

                    BOBBY JAY
          What would you've said?

                    NICK
          I don't know...

Nick is mesmerized by the sizzling cheese on Bobby Jay's pie.

                    NICK
          ...I'd just like him to feel immeasurable
          pain and humiliation.

                    BOBBY JAY
               (Joking)
          That'd be kinda tough, I mean he's
          already a Senator.

Polly chuckles, but Nick is lost in thought.

                    POLLY
          I mean, how would you get back in even if
          you wanted to?...

Nick looks at his fellow mod squad members and smiles.

                    BOBBY JAY
          Uh oh.

88.

INT. SENATOR FINISTIRRE'S OFFICE - DAY

The Senator is at his desk, examining a list, when Ron Goode
enters...

                    RON GOODE
          You're not going to like this.

Ron turns on the TV - Nick at a PRESS CONFERENCE.

                    NICK (ON TV)
          ... To all the people who were mentioned
          in the recent newspaper article, please
          take comfort in knowing that I will not
          rest until your names are cleared. This
          experience has taught me an important
          lesson...

INT. HEATHER HOLLOWAY'S OFFICE, WASHINGTON PROBE - DAY

We push into Heather as she realizes Nick is on a nearby TV.

                    NICK (ON TV)
          Having sexual affairs with members of the
          press is just unfair. Not unfair to me
          mind you, but to all the people in my
          life whose only crime is knowing me.

Heather notices her colleagues gathering around the TV.

                    NICK (ON TV)(CONT'D)
          It was your names, not mine, that
          suffered from my entertaining of a
          meaningless affair with a seductress in
          the form of a young brunette Washington
          reporter, whose name I won't mention,
          because I... have dignity.

Heather gulps.

EXT. PRESS CONFERENCE - DAY

A reporter speaks up. We recognize him as the TRAINEE from
the Academy, that Nick obviously planted in the crowd.

                    TRAINEE
          Ahem, Mr. Naylor. Do you still plan on
          testifying at tomorrow's subcomittee
          hearing on tobacco?

                    NICK
          I'm glad you asked that question.

The trainee smiles.

                    NICK (CONT'D)
          There have been wide accusations of me
          dropping out from tomorrow's hearing...

INT. SENATOR FINISTIRRE'S OFFICE - DAY

Finistirre continues watching Nick on TV.

                    NICK (ON TV)
          Let it be known, that unless Senator
          Finistirre has withdrawn my invitation to
          speak...

                    FINISTIRRE
               (to TV)
          It's called a subpoena.

                    NICK (ON TV)
          ... it is my plan to be present in
          Congress tomorrow to share my knowledge
          of Big Tobacco and all those who enjoy
          its products. Thank you for your time.
          See you tomorrow.

As Nick steps away from the podium on TV, we turn around to
find Finistirre who stares at the television, feeling every
bit challenged.

As we get closer, a phone rings in the background. Then a
second line rings... A third.

The Senator looks to his desk, where his phone's many lines
are all blinking.

He goes to his desk, and pulls out a sheet that reads:

                    SCHEDULE OF EVENTS

                   Tobacco Subcommittee

He follows the sheet down, past a list of names. At the
bottom he adds the name, NICK NAYLOR.

EXT. DC SKYLINE - MORNING

The Sun bursts out from behind various monuments.

INT. CONGRESSIONAL HEARING ROOM - DAY

An AV OPERATOR plugs in a mic sitting on the RED TABLECLOTH
of the witnesses table. He gives a thumbs up. AV OPERATOR 2
turns on the P.A. system. The room comes alive with a *BOOM*.

EXT. THE CAPITAL BUILDING - DAY

From a limo window, we see the press quickly approaching, but
all we hear is the sound of an on-coming wave. As the press
hits the car, the wave sound crashes as if hitting a beach.

Inside the car are a very shocked Nick, Bobby Jay, and Polly.

                    BOBBY JAY
          Still feel like Jimmy Stewart?

INT. ENTRANCE - CAPITAL BUILDING - DAY

Nick and Polly walk through the metal detector. Bobby Jay
tries to walk through, but sets off the machine.

                    BOBBY JAY
                (to Nick and Polly)
          Go ahead. This may take a while.

A SECURITY GUARD approaches with the WAND. Bobby Jay has
nothing but disdain for metal detectors.

INT. CONGRESSIONAL HEARING ROOM - DAY

The hearing is just beginning. Senator Finistirre and ten of
his colleagues sit at a long bench before the audience.
Finistirre scans the audience, then begins.

                    FINISTIRRE
          Okay, let's bring this meeting to order.
          We'll try our best to keep everything
          brief and concise, so we can all make it
          out of here on time.

Finistirre smiles at his audience.

                    FINISTIRRE
          Okay...

INT. CONGRESSIONAL HEARING ROOM - MOMENTS LATER

A MEDICAL ADVISOR is testifying.

                    MEDICAL ADVISOR
          The skull and crossbones means one thing:
          Poison. Thus, the message is quite clear.
          Like any other product that carries the
          branding, if you take it, you will die.

                    FINISTIRRE
          Yes, but isn't this overkill? I mean, why
          not just use words as we currently do?
          Something that describes the dangers of
          cigarettes?

                    MEDICAL ADVISOR
          The American public is not affected by
          mast head anymore. They need photographs.
          We've done studies which show that
          consumers react up to eighty percent more
          to imagery rather than words.

The Senator pretends to be entertaining a revelation.

                    MEDICAL ADVISOR (CONT'D)
          The stats are there. It's just sad that
          the Academy of Tobacco Studies did not
          release this type of information
          earlier...

                    FINISTIRRE
          And when you say the Academy of Tobacco
          Studies, you are referring to the
          coalition represented by...

                    MEDICAL ADVISOR
          The cigarette industry...

                    FINISTIRRE
          Yes...?

                    MEDICAL ADVISOR
          And... the Academy... and um?

Finistirre continues to coax him.

                    FINISTIRRE
          And... specifically, Mr...?

                    MEDICAL ADVISOR
          Mr. Uh... Nick?

Finistirre nods.

                    MEDICAL ADVISOR (CONT'D)
          Mr. Nick Naylor.

                    FINISTIRRE
                    (immediately)
          Thank you very much.

INT. CONGRESSIONAL HEARING ROOM - MOMENTS LATER

                    LATINO MAN
          The current use of words instead of
          imagery is an obvious move against the
          non-English speaking population in the
          United States. The skull and crossbones
          speaks loudly in all languages. By not
          using it, they are saying they want those
          who can't read English to die.

                    FINISTIRRE
          I'm sorry Senor Herera, could you clarify
          "they"...

FREEZE FRAME on the Senator.

                    NICK (V.O.)
          Let it be known, the public beating has
          not gone out of style.

INT. CONGRESSIONAL HEARING ROOM - MOMENTS LATER

Finistirre looks down at his agenda and smiles.

                    FINISTIRRE
          Nick Naylor, please step forward.

Nick stands. He turns around as he fixes his suit coat. As he
does, he notices someone in the audience. Sitting ten rows
back is... Joey. The twelve year old sneaks an excited wave.
Nick suddenly becomes uncomfortable. He waves back, bothered.

                    FINISTIRRE
          Please state your name, address, and
          current occupation.

                    NICK
          My name is Nick Naylor. I live at 6000
          Massachusetts Avenue. I am currently
          unemployed, but until recently, I was the
          Vice President of the Academy of Tobacco
          Studies.

                    FINISTIRRE
          Mr. Naylor, as Vice President of the
          Academy of Tobacco Studies, what was
          required of you? What did you do?

                    NICK
          I informed the public of all the research
          performed in the investigation on the
          effects of tobacco.

                    FINISTIRRE
          And what, so far, has the Academy
          concluded in the investigation on the
          effects of tobacco?

                    NICK
          Well, many things actually. Why just the
          other day, they uncovered evidence that
          smoking can offset Parkinson's disease.

                    FINISTIRRE
          I'm sure the health community is thrilled.
          Mr. Naylor, Who provides the financial
          backing for the Academy of Tobacco Studies?

                    NICK
          Conglomerated Tobacco.

                    FINISTIRRE
               (clarifying)
          That is the cigarette companies?

                    NICK
          For the most part, yes.

                    FINISTIRRE
          Do you think this affects their
          priorities?

                    NICK
          No. Just as I'm sure campaign
          contributions don't affect yours.

Senator LOTHRIDGE from Washington pipes in, to break it up.

                    LOTHRIDGE
          Gentlemen, Mr. Naylor is not here to testify
          on the goings on of the Academy of Tobacco
          Studies. We're here to examine the possibility
          of a warning logo on cigarettes.
                    (MORE)

                    LOTHRIDGE (CONT'D)
      Now, Mr. Naylor, I have to ask out of
      formality, do you believe that smoking
      cigarettes over time can lead to lung cancer
      and other respiratory conditions such as
      emphysema?

Finistirre rolls his eyes. (*What do you think*?)

A long pause, as Nick searches through everything. The people
in the room. The people watching on television.

                    NICK
      Yes.

Finistirre looks up in astonishment as the whole room suddenly
bustles with energy. Polly and Bobby Jay exchange glances.

                    NICK
      In fact, I think you'd be hard pressed to
      find someone who really believes that
      cigarettes are not potentially harmful.
         (turns to audience)
      I mean, show of hands...

                    LOTHRIDGE
      Mr. Naylor, there is no need for
      theatrics.

                    NICK
      I'm sorry, I just don't see the point in
      a warning label for something people
      already know.

Senator DUPREE from Michigan speaks up.

                    DUPREE
      The warning symbol is a <u>reminder</u>. A
      reminder of the dangers of smoking
      cigarettes.

                    NICK
      Well, if we want to remind people of
      danger, why don't we slap a skull and
      crossbones on all Boeing Airplanes,
      Senator Lothridge...

We notice Lothridge's name plate says (D) WASHINGTON.

                    NICK
      ... and all Fords, Senator Dupree.

Dupree's name plate says (R) MICHIGAN.

                    FINISTIRRE
          That's just ridiculous. The death toll on
          passenger planes and car fatalities
          doesn't even skim the surface of
          cigarettes. They don't even compare.

                    NICK
          Oh, this from a Senator who calls
          Vermont, home.

Finistirre raises an eyebrow.

                    LOTHRIDGE
          I don't follow you, Mr. Naylor.

                    NICK
          Well, the real demonstrated number-one
          killer in America is cholesterol.

Still stares. Nick continues.

                    NICK (CONT'D)
          And here comes Senator Finistirre, whose
          fine state is, I regret to say, clogging
          the nation's arteries with Vermont cheddar
          cheese.

A rumble through the crowd.

                    NICK (CONT'D)
          If you want to talk numbers, how about the
          millions of people dying of heart attacks.
          Perhaps Vermont cheddar should come with a
          skull and crossbones.

                    FINISTIRRE
               (can hardly contain himself)
          Why you... The Great State of Vermont
          will not apologize for its cheese.

This garners odd looks from his fellow Senators.

Nick looks back at Joey who gives him the thumbs up.

                    LOTHRIDGE
          Mr. Naylor, we are here to discuss
          cigarettes. Not any other products. Now, as
          discussed earlier, these warning labels are
          not for those who know, but rather for
          those who don't. What about the children?

                    NICK
        Gentlemen, it's called education. It doesn't
        come off the side of a cigarette carton. It
        comes from our teachers and more importantly
        our parents. It is the job of every parent to
        warn their children of all the dangers of the
        world, including cigarettes. So one day, when
        they get older, they can choose for themselves.

Nick looks back at his son.

                    NICK (CONT'D)
        I look at my son, who was kind enough to
        come with me today, and I can't help
        think of myself as responsible for his
        growth and his development. And I'm proud
        of that.

                    FINISTIRRE
        In that case, Mr. Naylor, would you
        condone him smoking?

                    NICK
        Of course not, he's not eighteen. That
        would be illegal.

                    FINISTIRRE
        Yes, I heard you deliver the same
        response on 20/20. But enough dancing.
        What about when he does turn eighteen?

Nick is momentarily speechless.

                    FINISTIRRE (CONT'D)
        Come on Mr. Naylor? On his eighteenth
        birthday, will you share a cigarette? Enjoy
        the afternoon like one of those sick tobacco
        advertisements? You certainly have a lot to
        say on how we should raise our children.
        What of your own? What are you going to do
        when he turns eighteen?

Joey looks to his father.

Nick looks up at the various senators. He takes a breath.

                    NICK
        If he really wants a cigarette... I'll
        buy him his first pack.

Joey smiles proudly.

Finistirre rocks back.

                    FINISTIRRE
          Thank you for your testimony, Mr. Naylor.
          You're excused

Nick nods and stand up to leave. He nods to Joey on the way.

INT. MAIN FOYER, CAPITAL BUILDING - DAY

Nick steps into an empty room. He takes in what just happened
for a moment. Out of nowhere, BR saddles up next to him - All
smiles. He grabs Nick's shoulder.

                    BR
          Well done, my boy!

Nick looks over, confused. *My boy?*

                    NICK
          Were you in the same room as me?

                    BR
          The whole personal choice thing. They ate
          that shit up. Just checked the whip
          count. The bill is going down in flames.
          Your speech was... unorthodox, but you
          did it... You crushed the fucker.

                    NICK
          That's great news for you guys.

                    BR
          Hey, now. We're still a team, right?

                    NICK
          What about, "damage control"?

Nick and BR stop at the MAIN DOORS. The crowd waiting on the
other side.

                    BR
               (levels with him)
          Look, Nick. Winston-Salem is ready to do
          whatever it takes to keep you on board...

Nick thinks for a moment, then smiles.

EXT. THE MAIN STEPS, CAPITAL BUILDING - DAY

Nick and his son Joey stand on the main steps, surrounded by
reporters. Joey looks to his dad with pride.

> REPORTER 1
> Nick, will you continue fighting for
> cigarettes?

BR enters and puts his arm around Nick.

> BR
> Of course he will! This man here is our
> general. We're not going to just let him
> retire.

> REPORTER 2
> Is that correct, Nick? You're sticking
> with tobacco?

Nick goes to say something, when we FREEZE FRAME.

> NICK (V.O.)
> Now, I know what you're probably
> thinking. What a great opportunity for me
> to teach Joey how to use leverage against
> a back-stabbing boss.

We see Joey looking on thoughtfully. BR grinning.

                                              CUT TO:

NICK AND JOEY IN THE CAR IN CALIFORNIA

Nick looks over to his son.

> NICK (V.O.)
> But I actually meant what I said about
> responsibility. Something's are just more
> important than paying the mortgage...

                                              BACK TO:

EXT. STEPS OF CONGRESS - DAY

Nick talks to the press.

> NICK
> So, I did the only responsible thing I
> could... I turned down the job.

BR's eyes look as if they're about to burst.

                    NICK (V.O.)
          And my timing couldn't have been better.

                                        CUT TO:

NEWS FOOTAGE OF THE GREAT AMERICAN TOBACCO SETTLEMENT

Various people testify on the witness stands. Tobacco
executives hang their heads in shame. An attorney shows off a
GIANT CHECK.

                    NICK
          Within a few months, the cigarette
          companies settled with the American
          smokers to the tune of two hundred forty
          six billion dollars

EXT. ACADEMY OF TOBACCO STUDIES - DAY

A WORKMAN chips the LETTERS off of the Academy's sign.

                    NICK (V.O.)
          The Academy for Tobacco Studies was
          permanently dismantled.

INT. BR'S OFFICE - ACADEMY OF TOBACCO STUDIES - DAY

BR packs a box with his possessions. He looks fondly at a
Plexiglas trophy, shaped like a cigarette.

                    NICK (V.O.)
          For the first time in decades, BR found
          himself out of work.

INT. BERT'S RESTAURANT - DAY

The MOD squad meets at their table.

                    NICK (V.O.)
          Otherwise, not much has changed. The MOD
          squad still meets every week.

Pull out to reveal three new members.

                    NICK (V.O.)
          We even added a few new members.

New ICONS appear above each of the members' heads. Oil.
Nuclear Waste. Fast Food.

INT. HOLLYWOOD PENETRATION INTERVIEW - DAY

                    NICK (V.O.)
          Senator Finistirre is still fighting for
          his causes.

Finistirre is interviewed by a plastic HOLLYWOOD INTERVIEWER.
The name of the show reads, "Hollywood Penetration".

                    HOLLYWOOD INTERVIEWER
          What do you say to the people who claim
          you are destroying cinema classics?

                    FINISTIRRE
          All we are doing is using digital
          technology to tastefully update movies of
          the past... By removing cigarettes.

FLASH IMAGES: Classic Hollywood stars holding new objects
instead of cigarettes... a party blower... a carrot... a
candy cane... a mug of coffee.

                    FINISTIRRE
          I believe that if these stars were alive
          today, they'd agree we are doing the
          right thing.

                    HOLLYWOOD INTERVIEWER
          But in essence, aren't you changing
          history?

                    FINISTIRRE
          No... I think we're improving history.

The interviewer blinks twice - *Are you shitting me?*

EXT. BEACH SIDE - DEAD OF NIGHT

                    NICK (V.O.)
          Even Heather is still reporting.

LEVEL 5 HURRICANE.

All we see is Heather in a blue parka, lit by the camera
man's SPOTLIGHT, desperately trying to report through the
sheets of RAIN and 90 mile-an-hour WIND.

                    HEATHER
          ... The whole town has been evacuated.
          They're calling this the storm of the...

"WHAM!" - A flying PALM FROND smacks Heather in the face, knocking her to the ground.

                                                    CUT TO:

INT. SCHOOL THEATER - DAY

We find nick, Polly, and Bobby Jay sitting near the back, surrounded by parents who look forward anxiously.

                    NICK (V.O.)
              Not much changes at all.

                    DEBATE MODERATOR (O.C.)
              And this year's debate champion is...

Reveal the DEBATE MODERATOR standing on stage at a podium in a tweed coat and bow tie. He holds up a card and a trophy.

                    DEBATE MODERATOR
              ... Joey Naylor!

Joey appears from stage left, beaming. He runs up and accepts his trophy as Nick, Polly, and Bobby Jay burst into applause.

                                                    CUT TO:

INT. OFFICE CORRIDOR - DAY

Nick steps through a doorway and fixes his tie.

                    NICK (V.O.)
              And me...?

Nick closes the door behind him and exits frame, revealing a placard: "NAYLOR STRATEGIC RELATIONS".

                    NICK (V.O.)
              There's still a place for guys like me.

INT. BOARD ROOM - UNKNOWN COMPANY - DAY

Nick faces three GENTLEMEN in nice suits.

                    NICK
              So, be straight with me. Is it true?

Obvious embarrassment and confusion around the table.

                    GENTLEMEN 1
              It could be.

                    GENTLEMEN 2
          Well, we don't quite know that. It's
          complicated.

                    GENTLEMEN 3
          Very few cases, really.

                    NICK
          Look, gentlemen. Practice these words in
          front of a mirror: 'Although we are
          constantly exploring the subject,
          currently, there is no direct evidence that
          links cell phone usage to brain cancer.'

The gentlemen smile to each other. They've found their man.

Push into Nick. He looks straight at camera and smiles.

                    NICK (V.O.)
          Michael Jordan plays ball. Charles Manson
          kills people. I talk.

Nick winks.

                    NICK (V.O.)
          Everyone has a talent.

Black.

CAST AND CREW CREDITS

FOX SEARCHLIGHT PICTURES and ROOM 9 ENTERTAINMENT Present
A DAVID O. SACKS Production
In Association With CONTENTFILM
A JASON REITMAN Film

AARON ECKHART

THANK YOU FOR SMOKING

MARIA BELLO CAMERON BRIGHT ADAM BRODY SAM ELLIOTT KATIE HOLMES
DAVID KOECHNER ROB LOWE WILLIAM H. MACY J.K. SIMMONS AND ROBERT DUVALL

Written for the Screen and
Directed by
JASON REITMAN

Producer
DAVID O. SACKS

Based on the Novel by
CHRISTOPHER BUCKLEY

Executive Producers
PETER THIEL
ELON MUSK
MAX LEVCHIN
MARK WOOLWAY
EDWARD R. PRESSMAN
JOHN SCHMIDT
ALESSANDRO CAMON

Executive Producer / UPM
MICHAEL BEUGG

Director of Photography
JAMES WHITAKER

Production Design by
STEVE SAKLAD

Editor
DANA E. GLAUBERMAN

Co-Executive Producer
DAVID J. BLOOMFIELD

Co-Producers
DANIEL BRUNT
DANIEL DUBIECKI

Co-Producer / Casting Director
MINDY MARIN

Co-Producer
MICHAEL R. NEWMAN

Composer
ROLFE KENT

Music Supervisors
PETER AFTERMAN
MARGARET YEN

Costume Designer
DANNY GLICKER

Associate Producers
EVELEEN ANNE BANDY
STEPHEN BELAFONTE

Assistant Editor
ROBERT MALINA

CAST

Herself	JOAN LUNDEN
Robin Williger	ERIC HABERMAN
Nick Naylor	AARON ECKHART
Sue Maclean.	MARY JO SMITH
Ron Goode	TODD LOUISO
Kidnapper	JEFF WITZKE
BR	J.K. SIMMONS
Teacher . .	MARIANNE MUELLERLEILE
Joey Naylor	CAMERON BRIGHT
Kid # 1	ALEX DIAZ
Kid # 2	JORDAN GARRETT
Kid #3.	COURTNEY BURNESS
Kid #4	JORDAN ORR
Polly Bailey	MARIA BELLO
Bobby Jay Bliss	DAVID KOECHNER
Jill Naylor.	KIM DICKENS
Brad	DANIEL TRAVIS
Senator Ortolan Finistirre	WILLIAM H. MACY
Jeanette	KATIE WINSLOW
Trainee	RICHARD SPEIGHT, JR.
Tobacco Club Host .	ERIC MALDONADO
Captain.	ROBERT DUVALL
Tiffany	RENEE GRAHAM
Heather Holloway	KATIE HOLMES
Jack.	ADAM BRODY
EGO Assistant. . .	TIMOTHY DOWLING
Jeff Megall	ROB LOWE
Lorne Lutch	SAM ELLIOTT
Pearl.	CONNIE RAY
Himself	DENNIS MILLER
Ski Mask #1	TERRY JAMES
Ski Mask #2	MARC SCIZAK
Flighty Girl	RACHEL THORP
Nurse	KAREN HARRISON
Doctor	AARON LUSTIG

Interviewer	MELORA HARDIN
Voice of F.B.I. Agent	BRIAN PALERMO
Dr. Meisenbach	MICHAEL MANTELL
Mr. Herera	TONYO MELENDEZ
Senator Lothridge	SPENCER GARRETT
Senator Dupree	EARL BILLINGS
Reporter #1	CATHERINE REITMAN
Reporter #2	SEAN PATRICK MURPHY
Oil Lobbyist	DAVID O. SACKS
Herself	NANCY HUMPRIES O'DELL
Debate Moderator	ROY JENKINS
Gentleman #1	HOWARD WEITZMAN
Gentleman #2	BRUCE FRENCH
Gentleman #3	ROBERT L. RICHARDS
Stunt Coordinator	TERRY JAMES
Stunts	MARC SCIZAK

CREW

Unit Production Manager
.... MICHAEL BEUGG
First Assistant Director
.... JASON A. BLUMENFELD
Second Assistant Director
.... SONIA BHALLA
Associate Producers
.... EVELEEN ANNE BANDY
STEPHEN BELAFONTE
Production Supervisor
.... BOB DOHRMANN
Second Unit Director of Photography
..... NICOLE HIRSCH-WHITAKER
Camera Operator/Steadicam Operator
.... TOMMY LOHMANN
Camera Operator ... DANIEL NICHOLS
First Assistant Camera
.... DONALD BURGHARDT
Second Assistant Camera.. BRETT GATES
Additional Steadicam Operators
.... COLIN HUDSON
KENJI LUSTER
"B" Camera 1st Assistant .. JOSH MEDAK
Loaders .... TIM CLARKE
ANDREW DEPUNG
Production Sound Mixer.... STEVEN A.
MORROW, C.A.S.
Boom Operator... CRAIG DOLLINGER
Utility Sound.... ROBERT SHARMAN
BRAD BRYAN
Video Assist Operators ... PETE ALBERT
MICHAEL BAIRD
BOB STERRY
Still Photographer... DALE ROBINETTE
Gaffer .... PACKY LENNON

Best Boy Electric
.... KONRAD SIGURDSSON
Electricians ... PATRICK M. BRENNAN
RALPH COON
TIM GILLIS
PHIL HARDT
RUDY MARTINEZ
VLADIMIR TAMAYO
Second Second Assistant Directors
.... CASEY MAKO
SCOTT BROWN
Location Manager
...... CHRISTOPHER D. MILLER
Key Assistant Location Manager
.... MICHAEL CHICKEY
Location Scouts.... ERROL REICHOW
RON SHINO
Script Supervisor MARY ANNE SEWARD
Casting Assistants .. EMBER TRUESDELL
CATHY WEINER
Extras Casting
.. SMITH & WEBSTER-DAVIS CASTING
TAMMY L. SMITH
DIXIE WEBSTER-DAVIS
Assistant Art Director
.... STEVEN SAMANEN
Art Department Coordinator
.... THERESA GREENE
Set Decorator
...... KURT MEISENBACH, S.D.S.A.
Leadman .. PAUL ARTHUR HARTMAN
Key Set Dresser... GREG O'DONOHUE
On Set Dressers ..... MARK BROOKS
OTIS KALTVEDT
Swings .... M. MARCOS GONZALEZ
GREG O'DONOHUE
Property Master .. NEAL W. ZOROMSKI
Assistant Property Master
.... OLIVER DOERING
Storyboard Artist .... EDDIE LIN
Construction Consultant
.... MICHAEL CROWE
Construction Foreman
.... GLENN WILLIAMS
Paint Foreman ...... PHIL BRANDES
Prop Makers...... CASEY GARRETT
KEVIN WENGER
Special Effects Coordinator
.... LARRY FIORITTO
Special Effects Technician
.... VIRGIL SANCHEZ
Costume Supervisor
.... JULIE GLICK GLICMAN
Key Set Costumer .. LAURA LIZ LITTLE

Set Costumer . . . MARTA VILLALOBOS
Department Head Makeup Artist
. . . . JOHN E. JACKSON
Department Head Hair Stylist
. . . . MARSHA LEWIS
Key Hair Stylist . . . . MAXINE MORRIS
Mr. Eckhart's Makeup Artist
. . . . ELISABETH FRY
Mr. Duvall's Makeup Artist . . ROBIN LUCE
Key Grip . . . STUART M. ABRAMSON
Best Boy Grips . . . . . DEANO MANLEY
DANIEL Q. REILLY
Dolly Grip . . . . . SHAWN STODDARD
Grips . . . . TONY AYALA
GARY C. BEAIRD
MIKE DELNERO
TOM LAMONT
ALEX REILLY
BLAKE SANTORO
ROBERT SANTORO
Clearance Coordinator
. . . . ASHLEY KRAVITZ
Production Office Coordinator
. . . . TRACEIGH SCOTTEL
Assistant Production Office Coordinators
. . . . TARA L. CRAIG
KELLY LEE MCCORMICK
MICHYL-SHANNON QUILTY
Production Office Assistants
. . . . FRANCIS M. HADINOTO
ALYSSA HOUZE
NICKOLAS YOUNKER
Cast Production Assistant . . . PAUL BOCK
Key Set Production Assistant
. . . . PATRICK CUNNINGHAM
Set Production Assistants . . . NINO ALDI
JENNIFER BUONANTONY
JOE DORNICH
UDAY SHARAD JOSHI
Production Accountant
. . . . GAVIN J. BEHRMAN
First Assistant Accountants . . AMY SMOLEV
JILL ROSENBLATT
Payroll . . . . . . STEPHANIE WESCOTT
Stand-Ins . . . AARON "AJ" RICHMOND
MICHELLE SHORE
KATIE WINSLOW
Set Medics . . . . MIKE ARTINO
DAVID FALICKI
PATRICE M. KING
Transportation Coordinator
. . . . GENO HART
Transportation Captain . . RICK FESE, JR.

Transportation Co-Captains
. . . . JOE COSENTINO
. . . . DENNIS JANOVICI
Transportation Clerk
. . . . NATHAN M. HARD.C.CASTLE
Drivers   MICHAEL R. BELT
NEIL CHISHOLM
JON R. COSHAM
LEE JENNINGS
JERRY KNIGHT
ROGELIO M. LOERA
MICHAEL L. "BUD" RUBEN
CARLOS M. SERRANO
WILLIAM SMALLWOOD
JOSEPH TAGGART
SCOTT TYLER
GLYNN WILLIAMS
Mr. Eckhart's Driver . . . JOSH SARFATY
Studio Teacher . . . . . JULIE STEVENS
Assistant to Mr. Eckhart . . VALARIE PAYNE
Assistant to Mr. Reitman
. . . . . . PHILLIP MONTGOMERY
Assistant to Mr. Sacks . . JEFFREY WANK
Assistant to Mr. Sacks – Post Production
. . . . ADAM ZADIKOFF
Craft Service . . . NATHAN MARUCCIO
Craft Service Assistant
. . . . CARMELO RANDAZZO
Catering
. . . . . CAST AND CREW CATERING
Chef . . . . . . GENARO RODRIGUEZ
First Assistant . . . . . . JAIME RAMIREZ
Second Assistants . . . . LUIS CABRERA
CARLOS RODRIGUEZ

WASHINGTON D.C. UNIT
Second Assistant Director
. . . . XANTHUS VALAN
Camera Operator . . . . . DAVID INSLEY
Second Assistant Camera . . . . STU STEIN
Loader . . . . . . CHARLIE NEWBERRY
Best Boy Electric . . . . TED AYD
Electricians . . . . TIM GORDON
KENNETH H. HARRIS
Key Grip . . . . DEAN CITRONI
Best Boy Grip . . . . . RICK STRODEL
Dolly Grip . . . . RHETT BLOOMQUIST
Grips . . . . MICHAEL O'LEARY
LEE SHAPIRA
Costume Supervisor . . . . . DEB DALTON
Set Costumer . . . . . JOAN M. LYNCH
Key Hair Stylist . . SHERRI BRAMLETT
Assistant Property Master
. . . . ERIC HUNSAKER

Leadman . . . . CARL CATANESE
On Set Dresser
. . . . STEPHEN G. SHIFFLETTE
Production Sound Mixer . . LEN SCHMITZ
Boom Operator. . . . . . PAUL FLINTON
Casting
. . . . BETSY ROYALL CASTING, C.S.A.
Location Manager . . JOHN LATENSER V
Assistant Location Manager
. . . . JONATHAN REICH
Locations Production Assistant
. . . . MATTHEW D. NOONAN
Second Second Assistant Director
. . . . KURT UEBERSAX
Production Consultant
. . . . JONATHAN ZURER
Production Associate
. . . . DREW VANDERVELDE
Assistant Production Associate
. . . . LISA HAGENMEYER
Office Production Assistant
. . . . CHRISTOPHER GEAIR
Set Production Assistants. . . DANA LEWIS
ASA MCCALL
MELISSA MORGAN
GREGORY S. PURCELL
Medic . . . . JEFF JOHNSON
Craft Services . . . . TOM CORNELIUS
Craft Services Assistant . . . JULIE BRIGGS
Catering
. . . . BLACK DIAMOND CATERING
Catering Chef . . . PETER ROSKOVICH
First Assistant . . . . SAM ENNIS
Transportation Coordinator
. . . . GILBERT YOUNG
Dispatcher
. . . . . DANIELLE FREDERICKSON
Picture Car Coordinator
. . . . NELSON C. WRIGHT, JR.
Transportation Captain
. . . . VERDELL E. VENEY
Drivers . . . RALPH GORDON BLAINE
ANTHONY CANARD
DONALD DIGGS
STEPHEN MONAGHAN
EUGENE TILLMAN
GLEM WILLIAMS
JOHNNY WILLIAMS

JOAN LUNDEN SHOW
PRODUCTION UNIT
Camera Operators. . . . . . SCOTT KAYE
BRUCE OLDHAM
Jib Operator . . . . DON BERG

Video Technician. . . DEXTER PADGITT
Studio Liaison. . . . . MALISSA STRONG

DENNIS MILLER SHOW
PRODUCTION UNIT
Camera Operators . . KAREN IACOFANO
JOSEPH G. PIER
Video Technician
. . . . RICHARD R. CONIGLIO
Board Operator. . KAREN PERSECHINO
Stagehands. . . . . BOB CHURCH
FRANK ROSE
Production Consultant . . MIKE HAZLITT

POST PRODUCTION
First Assistant Editor/Visual Effects Editor
. . . . ROBERT MALINA
Post Production Consulting by EPC
. . . . JOE FINEMAN
Post Production Supervisor
. . . . MICHAEL TOJI
Music Coordinator . . . ALISON LITTON
Main Titles . . . SHADOWPLAY STUDIO
Main Title Designers. . . . . JENNY LEE
ARI SACHTER–ZELTZER
GARETH SMITH
Avid Assistant Editors . . CLAY RAWLINS
STEVE RICKERT
Editorial Intern . . . YANOSH CUGLOVE
Digital Intermediate by. . . . . . . EFILM
Digital Color Timer. . NATASHA LEONETT
Digital Intermediate Producer
. . . . LORENE SIMPSON
Digital Intermediate Editor
. . . . LISA TUTUNJIAN
Digital Colorist. . . . . . JACK LEWARS
Digital Intermediate Assistant Producer
. . . . ESTHER LEE
Digital Opticals . . . PATRICK CLANCEY
Digital Film Services by
. . . . . DIGITAL FILM WORKS, INC.
Visual Effects Supervisor/Producer
. . . . . COSMAS PAUL BOLGER, JR.
Senior 3D Artist . . . . EDWARD QUIRK
Compositing Artists . . ROBERT LUKACS
TOMMY TRAN
Production Coordinators
. . . . HEATHER IGNARRO
SHARON STETZEL
Film Technician . . AANAND SHRESTHA
Sound Editorial by . . . EARCANDY, INC.
Supervising Sound Editor
. . . . PERRY ROBERTSON

Co-supervising Sound Editor
. . . . SCOTT SANDERS, M.P.S.E.
Supervising ADR Editor
. . . . BARNEY CABRAL
Sound Editor. . . . . . RICHARD DWAN
Assistant Sound Editor
. . . . KEVIN A. ZIMMERMAN
ADR Recorded at WESTWIND MEDIA, LLC
ADR Mixer . . . . . . PAUL DRENNING
Foley Recorded at . . POST CREATIONS
Foley Mixer . . . . GEORDY SINCAVAGE
Foley Artists. . . . . . PATRICK CABRAL
CYNTHIA MERRILL
Re-Recording Stages Provided by. . TODD-AO
Re-Recording Mixers
. . . . MELISSA HOFMAN, C.A.S.
ADAM JENKINS, C.A.S.
J. STANLEY JOHNSTON, C.A.S.
Recordist . . . . . . ROBERT ALTHOFF
Music Editor . . . . NICK SOUTH
Temp Music Editor . . . . . CURT SOBEL
Color Timer. . . . . . STEVE SHERIDAN
Telecine . . . . NT VIDEO
Negative Cutter
. . MAGIC FILM AND VIDEO WORKS
Post Production Accountant
. . . . CHARACTER COUNTS
MANAGEMENT GROUP
BOB WEBER
Cranes by
. . . PANAVISION REMOTE SYSTEMS
Camera Dollies by . . . . . . J.L. FISHER
CHAPMAN/LEONARD STUDIO
EQUIPMENT, INC.
Lighting and Grip Equipment
. . . . LEONETTI COMPANY
STEVE ALTMAN
Completion Guarantor. . FILM FINANCES
DAVE BENNETT
Legal Services by . . . REDER & FEIG LLP
BENJAMIN R. REDER, ESQ
DEBBIE AXEL, ESQ
ERIC J. SPIEGELMAN, ESQ
NOOR AHMED
North American Sales Representative
. . WILLIAM MORRIS INDEPENDENT
CASSIAN ELWES
International Sales by
. . CONTENTFILM INTERNATIONAL
JAMIE CARMICHAEL
Unit Publicist
. . . JEREMY WALKER & ASSOCIATES
JEREMY WALKER
JESSICA GRANT

Insurance . . . . SPEARE/ACORDIA
MARK SPIVEY
Payroll Services
. . . . ENTERTAINMENT PARTNERS
Script Clearance
. . ACT ONE SCRIPT CLEARANCE, INC.
RAFFI PALOULIAN
Travel Services . . . . . . TRAVELCORPS

©2006 Twentieth Century Fox Film
Corporation in all territories except Italy,
France, Switzerland, Benelux, Portugal,
Scandinavia, Greece, Bulgaria,
Commonwealth of Independent States,
Iceland, Brazil, Korea, Japan and Spain.
© 2006 TCF Hungary Film Rights
Exploitation Limited Liability Company and
Twentieth Century Fox Film Corporation in
Brazil, Korea, Japan and Spain
©2006 TYFS Productions, LLC in Italy,
France, Switzerland, Benelux, Portugal,
Scandinavia, Greece, Bularia,
Commonwealth of Independent States and
Iceland.

TYFS Productions, LLC is the author and
creator of this motion picture for the purpose
of copyright and other laws in all countries
throughout the world.

"SMOKE, SMOKE, SMOKE THAT
CIGARETTE!"
Written by Merle Travis, Tex Williams
Performed by Tex Williams
And the Western Caravan
Courtesy of Capitol Records
Under license from
EMI Film & Television Music

"SANDS OF IWO JIMA"
Written by Victor Young
Courtesy of Paramount Pictures

"TWO BEAT OR NOT TWO BEAT"
Composed and Performed by
Curt Sobel and Gary Schreiner
Courtesy of Palisades Music Productions

"SMOOTHER THAN JAZZ"
Written and Produced by
Matt Messina

"SMOKE RINGS"
Written by Eugene Gifford, Ned Washington
Performed by The Mills Brothers
Courtesy of Columbia Records
By arrangement with
SONY BMG MUSIC ENTERTAINMENT

"THE JOAN LUNDEN SHOW THEME"
Written and Produced by
Matt Messina

"STUTTERING TODD"
Written by Danny Seim
Performed by Danny Seim
Of Monomena
Courtesy of Bridgetown Breaks Co.

"BOW TO CHINESE"
Composed and Performed by
Curt Sobel and Gary Schreimer
Courtesy of Palisades Music Productions

"LITTLE ORGAN FUGUE"
Written by Johann Sebastian Bach
Arranged by Ward Swingle
Performed by The Swingle Singers
Courtesy of Virgin Classics Limited
Under license from EMI Film & Television
Music

"MELODIC TANK"
Written by Kevin O'Connor
Performed by Talkdemonic
Courtesy of Bridgetown Breaks Co.

"GREENBACK DOLLAR"
Written by Hoyt Axton, Ken Ramsey
Performed by The Kingston Trio
Courtesy of Capitol Records
Under license from EMI Film & Television
Music

Still Image Courtesy of Battlegrounds,
Louisville, KY

Courtesy of BBC Motion Gallery
Corbis
Footage Courtesy of C-SPAN Archives

Photos by Getty Images

NBC News Archives

Photo credit of Attila the Hun is courtesy of
North Wind Picture Archives, Alfred, Maine

Photo credit of Genghis Khan is courtesy of
North Wind Picture Archives, Alfred, Maine

SANDS OF IWO JIMA Courtesy of
Paramount Pictures

John Wayne used with permission of Wayne
Enterprises, LP,
Newport Beach, CA 92663. All Rights
Reserved. www.wayneenterprises.com

The John Wayne Cancer Foundation's mission is to bring courage strength and grit to
the fight against cancer.
© 2005 John Chamberlain/Artists Rights
Society (ARS), New York

Gary Cooper Courtesy of MODA
Entertainment, Inc.

™ 2005 The Estate of Bette Davis by CMG
Worldwide, Inc.
www.BetteDavis.com

™2005 The Estate of Errol Flynn by CMG
Worldwide, Inc. www.CMGWorldwide.com

™ & 2005 Marlene, Inc., Courtesy of Global
Icons, LLC. All rights reserved.

Special Thanks
COREY ACKERMAN
JANE AND GREG CASTANIAS
CHRIS CONTE- THE DENNIS MILLER
SHOW
MANIE ELLIS – THE PROSPECT STU-
DIOS
JAGENE FUNK – SOAP TALK
MELISSA HAVARD
CHARD HURLEY
JAY LIEBERMAN – QUIXOTE STUDIOS
TODD MOLZ
ROBERT NEWMAN – U.S. DEPART-
MENT OF ENERGY
PETER ROBINSON
JIM ROUDEBUSH & LORI KILLAM –
PANAVISION, WOODLAND HILLS
DAVID TATE
PETER UHLMANN
DIANE UPSON – EASTMAN KODAK

JARED SCARDINA – CREATIVE
ENTERTAINMENT SERVICES
JEFFREY WIGAND
DISTRICT OF COLUMBIA – OFFICE
OF MOTION PICTURE AND TV
DEVELOPMENT
THE HAND PROP ROOM
HYATT REGENCY, CAPTIOL HILL,
WASHINGTON D.C.
JONES DAY
METROPOLITAN POLICE DEPART-
MENT – WASHINGTON D.C.
MONT BLANC
THE MONTECITO PICTURE COM-
PANY
NATIONAL PARK SERVICE –
NATIONAL CAPITAL REGION
ORGANIZATION OF AMERICAN
STATES
THE PEOPLE OF THE DISTRICT OF
COLUMBIA
UNITED STATES PARK POLICE
THINKFILM, INC. – WASHINGTON
D.C.
WASHINGTON METROPOLITAN
AREA TRANSIT AUTHORITY

American Humane Association monitored the animal action. No animal was harmed in the making of this film.

The events, characters and firms depicted in this motion picture are fictitious. Any similarity to actual persons, living or dead, or to actual events or firms is purely coincidental.

This motion picture is protected under the laws of the United States and other countries. Unauthorized duplication, distribution, or exhibition may result in civil liability and criminal prosecution.

BIOS

JASON REITMAN (Writer/Director)

Jason Reitman was born in Montreal on October 19, 1977. He was on his first film set *(Animal House)* 11 days later. The son of director Ivan Reitman, he spent most of his childhood on or around film sets, surrounded by the funniest human beings on Earth. He even appeared in cameos in many of his father's films *(Twins, Ghostbusters II, Kindergarten Cop, Dave,* and *Father's Day).*

By 10, he was making the typical short films with his dad's home video camera. At 13, he got his first job on a film crew, as production assistant on *Kindergarten Cop.* At 15, Reitman made an AIDS public service announcement with actors from his high school that went on to win many awards and play on network television. Reitman graduated high school in 1995 and went on to USC to study English. There, he became a member of the comedy troupe *Commedus Interuptus* and held a short stint as co-host of a morning radio show.

During his sophomore year in college, Reitman created a small collegiate desk calendar company that provided the budget for his first short film, *Operation.* The short comedy about kidney stealing went on to premiere at the 1998 Sundance Film Festival. At 19 years old, this made him one of the youngest directors ever to have a film at the festival.

This began a string of short films, including H@ (premiered at South by Southwest 1999), *In God We Trust* (premiered at Sundance 2000, went on to play Toronto, Edinburgh, U.S. Comedy Arts, New Directors/New Films at MoMA and won best short at many festivals including Los Angeles, Aspen, Austin, Seattle, Florida, Athens, the New York Comedy Festival, and Bumbershoot Festival), *Gulp* (premiered at Sundance 2001), and *Consent* (premiered at Aspen Shorts Fest 2004 and won awards at Aspen and Seattle). Reitman's short films have played in over a hundred film festivals worldwide. He was recently awarded U.S. Comedy Art's Breakthrough Director.

In early 2000, Reitman signed with the commercial production company Tate and Partners. In the five years since he began directing television advertising, he has received honors from the Cannes commercial awards, the Addys, as well as the highly coveted One Show. Selected clients include Heineken, Honda, Nintendo, BMW, Kyocera, Asics, Amstel Light, Baskin Robbins, GM, Burger King, and Dennys.

In beginning his professional career, Reitman fulfilled a lifelong dream by joining the Directors Guild of America; at that time he was the guild's second youngest member.

CHRISTOPHER BUCKLEY (Author)

Christopher Buckley is editor of *Forbes FYI* magazine and the author of eleven books, many of them national bestsellers, including *Thank You for Smoking.* He is the winner of the distinguished ninth annual Thurber Prize for American Humor. Buckley lives in Washington, D.C., with his wife and two children and dog, Duck.

THANK YOU FOR SMOKING

FOX SEARCHLIGHT PICTURES AND ROOM 9 ENTERTAINMENT PRESENT A DAVID O. SACKS PRODUCTION IN ASSOCIATION WITH CONTENTFILM A JASON REITMAN FILM AARON ECKHART "THANK YOU FOR SMOKING" MARIA BELLO CAMERON BRIGHT ADAM BRODY SAM ELLIOTT KATIE HOLMES DAVID KOECHNER ROB LOWE WILLIAM H. MACY J.K. SIMMONS AND ROBERT DUVALL CASTING BY MINDY MARIN, CSA COSTUME DESIGN BY DANNY GLICKER MUSIC SUPERVISORS PETER AFTERMAN MARGARET YEN MUSIC BY ROLFE KENT CO-PRODUCERS DANIEL BRUNT DANIEL DUBIECKI MINDY MARIN MICHAEL R. NEWMAN CO-EXECUTIVE PRODUCER DAVID J. BLOOMFIELD EDITOR DANA E. GLAUBERMAN PRODUCTION DESIGN BY STEVE SAKLAD DIRECTOR OF PHOTOGRAPHY JAMES WHITAKER EXECUTIVE PRODUCERS PETER THIEL ELON MUSK MAX LEVCHIN MARK WOOLWAY EDWARD R. PRESSMAN JOHN SCHMIDT ALESSANDRO CAMON MICHAEL BEUGG BASED ON THE NOVEL BY CHRISTOPHER BUCKLEY PRODUCED BY DAVID O. SACKS WRITTEN FOR THE SCREEN AND DIRECTED BY JASON REITMAN

R RESTRICTED UNDER 17 REQUIRES ACCOMPANYING PARENT OR ADULT GUARDIAN DOLBY LANGUAGE AND SOME SEXUAL CONTENT

www.foxsearchlight.com

FOX SEARCHLIGHT